WHAT'S NEXT?

The Playbook for Achievers Rethinking Their Career Path

How to Figure Yourself Out and Make a Decision That Works for You

Elena Rezanova

What's next?

The playbook for achievers rethinking their career path

Elena Rezanova

Copyright © 2024 Elena Rezanova

This work is registered with UK Copyright Service: Registration No: 284756396

All rights reserved. No part of this book may be reproduces in any form or by any means without the prior written consent of the author, excepting brief quotes in reviews.

Contact: hello@elena-rezanova.com

Book cover design by Jason Anscomb

To all the professionals out there who are forging their own paths, and especially to my husband, with whom I share the values of freedom and choice.

Table of Contents

Introduction 1
    You Are at the "What's Next?" Point. Why? 1
    Strategy for Effective Reflection 12

Part 1. Big Questions Time 15
    1. "Who Am I?" 15
    2. "What Is My Passion?" 35
    3. "What Do I Really Want and Where Am I Headed?" 60
    4. "So, What's Next?" 68
    5. Big Ifs 83
        "What If I Am Making a Mistake?" 83
        "What If It's Too Late to Change Something?" 91
        "What If I Am Not Good Enough?" 96

Part 2. Mastering Career Transitions 102
    6. Learn to Navigate Transitions and Make the Most of Them 103
    7. When Work Isn't Working: A Case Study 115
        A Message for Leaders and Companies 132

Conclusion 138

Introduction

You Are at the "What's Next?" Point. Why?

Lisa adjusted a few figures on the application form and reviewed her resume one last time before she was about to submit it for a newly opened position in her department. With a deep breath, she hovered over the 'Submit' button but hesitated, her finger suspended in air. To her own surprise, she found herself seriously questioning her desire for this new role. Not long ago, she would have jumped at the chance to compete for the position without any doubts, but now, something was off.

Lisa works as a marketing executive at a large international company. She is smart and driven, and she moved up the corporate ladder fast, picking up promotions and awards as she went. People know her for being creative and full of energy. Even with all her success, Lisa increasingly felt a nagging sense that something was missing. For the past ten years, Lisa always knew her goals, always had the next challenge to conquer, the next peak to climb. But now she was thinking, *"Is that what I really want to do? And, by the way, what exactly do I want?"*

On the same day, in a different corner of the world, freelance graphic designer Amir pressed a button on a coffee maker and plunged into questions he had been occupied with for the last few months. It had been four years since he became his own boss. Being both diligent and responsible, he had successfully established a reputation. However, over time, Amir began to feel that he was losing interest and often had to force himself to take on projects. He noticed that his work was starting to lack the passion that had defined his early career.

He couldn't pinpoint the exact moment when the spark faded, but today he finally came to the realisation that he had hit a plateau and he needed to do something about that. Yet, for the time being, he returned to his desk with his fourth cup of coffee that morning—he needed all the energy to tackle his current tasks. *"Do I want to be doing this in 10 years' time?"*

Meanwhile, in another city, Feng, a co-founder of a fintech startup, hadn't even had a chance for coffee yet. He was stuck in traffic while on a conference call with the office. It wasn't the first time he noticed that he was pretending to be more engaged than he was. The constant honking and city hustle outside matched the turmoil he felt inside.

He and his partner, Sarah, had built the company from the ground up, and their venture had caught the eye of a bigger tech conglomerate. They agreed to a merger, seeing it as a chance to scale up. But as the integration process unfolded, Feng noticed the vibrant startup culture fading. Months passed, and his discomfort grew. He realized he had drifted far from the core essence that initially drove him to entrepreneurship. *"Am I ready for something new?"* he asked himself, contemplating the path ahead amidst the noise and hustle of the city.

If these stories resonate with you, then you already know what it's like to be at a point when you realize that something needs to change, when you question yourself and your career. And you're not alone. Over the last 15 years, I've met thousands of people who have been right where you are, asking themselves the same things. Let's call them the Big Questions:

Is that what I really want to do?
Who am I?
Am I who I want to be?
What do I really want?
Am I using my full potential?
Is this a good use of my life?
Should I stay or should I go?

All these big questions indicate a turning point. A very special time in our career when we rethink our path and decide what comes next. This time is also often called a career crisis.

What Brings Us to the 'What's Next?' Moment?

Why do we start questioning our career after putting in so much effort? Sometimes it's due to external factors. For example, good news at work like getting a new job offer, a promotion, or an exciting opportunity can make you see your job in a new light. But it's not always positive things—issues at work, losing a job, a pandemic, or economic problems can create this fork in the road. Big changes in our personal lives, like getting married, having kids, or moving with our family, can also be pivotal for our career.

But often, the biggest catalyst comes from within. Maybe a new dream, ambition, or business idea starts brewing, or we reflect on a road we didn't take. Meeting someone living the life and career we dream of can be eye-opening. And of course, feeling unhappy, stuck, or like we've hit a dead end, or realizing our work is out of sync with who we are can trigger us to rethink our career path.

External triggers might strike unexpectedly, but internal triggers accumulate over time. This process can take months or even years until we fully grasp the weight of the big questions. Then comes the time to find the answers we seek. This process cannot be ignored or canceled once it has begun; we inevitably have to find our answers.

This Isn't a Mistake in Your Previous Planning

If you're dealing with these big questions, you might think that your career has gone off track somewhere. However, that's not always the case. The turning point doesn't automatically imply that we made a mistake in our previous career plans. It's just a non-linear career in a non-linear world, where one stage ends and another begins.

Many of us are used to thinking of a career as a linear, unbroken path—a straight line leading to success. This traditional perspective still influences us today. Many believe that to future-proof their career, they must define their path early on and stick to it unwaveringly, avoiding any deviations along the way. It doesn't work like this anymore.

Both our careers and the world around us are in a constant state of flux. The business scene is so unpredictable, and the old career paths from the industrial times just don't cut it anymore. I think back to 1997 when I graduated from college; the world was an entirely different place. Companies like Google didn't exist and the iPhone was still a decade away. The internet wasn't widely used at home, and I couldn't have imagined how drastically it would transform the job market, making all of us a part of a global talent pool. In a few years, we'll look back at 2024 and find it as odd as we do 1997 now.

No traditional plan can keep up with a world that's constantly and quickly changing. It's nearly impossible to predict the future with complete certainty, whether for individuals or globally. Even if we think we've found the right path, we're always evolving inside, while life keeps throwing unexpected changes our way. Turning points and transitions in our careers are just inevitable.

Who Is This Book For?

This book is created for you, people like Lisa, Amir, and Feng—driven achievers from different walks of life, whether you're an employee, manager, independent pro, or business owner. People who were rowing hard but suddenly stopped to question if they were even going in the right direction.

You're ambitious, and you take your work very seriously. You know how to make things happen. You strive to invest your life with meaning. You play big, and you're dedicated to always growing and getting better.

You're used to being in charge of your own growth, and a lot of you have built your success from the ground up. That's why those big questions and 'what's next' moments can catch you totally by surprise. Just take a look at my inbox and read a few random emails where people describe their feelings when entering the Big Question Time:

"What went wrong? Why am I no longer excited about what used to be great a year ago?"

"Others see a beautiful facade of my career but I even feel guilty for not being happy with what I've done.'

"I'm so lost. What am I missing?"

"I pretend to be a financial director, but in fact, I don't know who am I."

"The worst part is, I don't know what to do about it. I hate this feeling; I've always been certain about what I wanted."

"What is all this for? And where am I in this?"

"There's no one I can talk to about it; folks might just brush it off as me overreacting."

"I know what I don't want, but I don't have a single idea of what I want then!"

WHAT'S NEXT?

The 'what's next?' moment brings a rollercoaster of emotions: feeling puzzled, disoriented, and maybe even less proud of what you've achieved. The overall feeling is confusion. This confusion happens because we were never taught how to rethink our careers and navigate transitions. We were never told that this is normal. Our education and employment systems are stuck in the traditional linear model where you pick a path early on and stick to it for life. We haven't been equipped with the skills to navigate a career based on a deep understanding of who we are, what we really want, and what makes us come alive. As a result, we struggle and feel lost every time we reach a turning point and face the big questions.

But since our careers naturally involve a series of transitions, we should expect, embrace, and learn how to navigate them. Even more, we can learn how to make the most of them! Every 'what's next' moment is a great chance to step back from our busy schedules and look within and around ourselves. After years of helping people through these times, I see it's not a time of crisis; it's a time of crystallization. It's a period for figuring out what truly brings us fulfillment and meaning. In fact, it helps us manage our careers with more clarity and intent, and we will learn this skill together.

Where Did This Book Come From?

This book comes from my two decades in the career development field, particularly from my international practice as a career strategist working with individuals. In this role, I've seen firsthand the ups and downs people experience in their careers, especially at those 'what's next?' moments. Being in the thick of it as a practitioner, I've seen them feel disoriented and lost, make tough choices, go through changes, and, step by step, craft their way forward.

As a specialist, I've pursued my own major questions: How do we find our path? How do we figure out what's right for us? Watching people struggle through career transitions, I keep asking myself: Why is this so hard and draining? Are there ways to make it easier, to avoid common mistakes?

It's especially upsetting when driven and high-potential people get stuck in their 'what's next?' phase for a long time. When this happens, it's not just a personal issue. It's tough for companies when valuable employees become 'quiet quitters'— those who show up to work but aren't fully present. Businesses miss out on talent, and talents miss out on opportunities. Nobody wins.

My own questions have driven me to explore this topic in depth. I've collected insights bit by bit, from both my practice and science. Career turning points and transitions have become my workplace, my habitat; this is the territory that I have been mapping for many years with all its abysses and shortcuts, where I meet people like Lisa, Amir, and Feng.

It's surreal to think that fifteen years ago, I was sure that career development wasn't my true passion. Back then, I worked in the talent department of a global company, grappling with my big questions and a sense of missing out. In 2011, we moved to France because my husband had started his education as a chef de cuisine, pursuing his dream after several successful years in trade marketing. My only understanding at that time was that I wanted something entirely different than people development—maybe becoming a photographer.

Our own big transition began, and during its ups and downs—really deep downs—my interest in my previously unloved profession suddenly reignited. Professional curiosity did that. I discovered that real-life wayfinding and transitions are far from what we typically expect and much different from what we know from books and success stories. They're contentious, lengthy, and exhausting, even if they bring us closer to our dreams. I often thought at that time, how could I not have known this when the topic of career development had been my main focus? But maybe it was for the best. Who knows, if our transition had been a breeze, I'd probably be processing photos now.

How Everything Is Set Up for You Here

This book is structured around the big questions we encounter at our "What's Next?" moments. My job is to help you find your unique answers to these questions and make choices that work for you.

WHAT'S NEXT?

We start with *"Who am I?"*—perhaps the most existential question. We'll explore your sense of self and what makes you, you. (My editor expressed some concern about immediately throwing you into deep work, but I know who I'm dealing with. I know that you've been looking for an answer for a long time and are tired of this search.)

Moving on to chapter two, we face another significant question: *"What is my passion?"* Here, we'll debunk all the myths and pitfalls surrounding passions and calling. We'll look at how people discover what makes them feel alive, where it comes from, what our dreams indicate, and what happens when we have those light bulb moments of "this is it!"

In the third chapter, *"What do I really want?"* we'll dive into figuring out where you're headed and how to discover your true ambitions. It's all about finding your North Star—the sense of direction and purpose that guides you.

The next chapter *"So, what's next?"* focuses on that crucial moment of making a choice. Here, you'll discover various approaches to figuring out your next move. We'll explore how changes can happen quickly or slowly and provide strategies to prevent you from getting stuck in your own thoughts when it's time to make a decision.

Then we're going to shift gears from *Big Questions* to *Big Doubts* – a natural and expected part of the journey.

Chapter five, *"Big Ifs"* addresses the common fear of making the wrong decision. We'll dive into and tackle the three big questions that arise on the threshold of career changes: *"What if I am making a mistake?"*
"What if it's too late to change something?"
"What if I am not good enough for that?"

Moving on to the second part of the book, *"Mastering career transitions"* we'll shift our focus from your current turning point to the bigger picture, viewing 'what's next?' moments as strategic opportunities. In this section, I'll guide you through strategies and tools to make the most of these opportunities.

In chapter 7 *"When Work Isn't Working: A Case Study"* we'll examine a case study of a successful yet unhappy professional. We'll dive into this story to unpack how our sense of happiness at work operates, and how we often overlook many important aspects of our work life. After this chapter, you'll start seeing your situation from a whole new perspective.

I want this book (and myself) to be your thinking partner—understanding and supportive, right by your side through your 'what's next?' moments.

While writing this book, I pictured you taking it along and setting aside a week or two for reflection. But it doesn't have to be like that. You might read it in the evenings, on weekends, or even at 3 AM when those big, nagging questions keep you awake. This book isn't a cure for insomnia (I hope), but it's here to remind you that you're not alone and that many others have been there and made it through.

I hope this book doesn't just provide answers but also sparks new and meaningful questions in your mind. Feel free to pause whenever you encounter something that truly resonates with you. My wish is that you'll find plenty of moments like that throughout the book. I suggest keeping a pen and notebook or notes app nearby while reading to jot down your thoughts and insights. Take time to really think about the important things that come up. Big answers don't rush to greet you; they tend to sneak up, slowly making sense as you move forward, layering in detail and depth.

So, with this in mind, I'm excited to welcome you aboard this journey. Let's discover what's next for you!

The Strategy for Effective Reflection

This book is packed with tools to help you uncover your personal insights on Big Questions. They aren't easy to answer; otherwise, people wouldn't spend months or even years trying to figure them out. The thing is, they require a certain approach.

Here I'll introduce you to the most effective method for tackling the questions presented here. This approach is backed by scientific research[1] and has been proven time and again in real-life scenarios.

This technique isn't just for career-related issues, either; it's a valuable tool for addressing complex questions in any aspect of your work or life. Turn to it whenever you are creating new products, finding solutions, and brainstorming ideas.

Three-stage process for getting good answers to big, complex questions:

1. Focus—IMMERSION

   Focus on the question, start by brainstorming, and write down your first ideas and answers.

2. Unfocus—INCUBATION

   Take a step back and give your mind a break from the question. This is when new fragments of answers may emerge, along with fresh ideas or perhaps even unexpected insights.

3. Refocus—CONSOLIDATION

   Re-focus your attention and summarize your thoughts into a cohesive answer.

Usually, people stop at the first stage, trying to get all possible answers out of their heads. But the real work happens in the second stage. The incubation period is particularly crucial when reflecting on complex questions. It lets your brain's natural thinking process (default mode network) work its magic. The best techniques for incubation include going for a walk (especially powerful for thinking), switching to a different task, or doing something fun and relaxing. As you try these, you'll discover what works best for you.

WHAT'S NEXT?

This three-step process can take anywhere from less than an hour to several days. Remember, there's no rush—enjoy your thinking journey.

Part 1. Big Questions Time

Chapter 1. Who Am I?

"I Don't Feel Like Myself Anymore"

As we started our first session on Zoom, Amir's face revealed both curiosity and a bit of unease. You already met him at the beginning of the book; he is a freelance graphic designer. With a deep breath, he shared, "I don't feel like myself anymore, like something's off."

I leaned into the screen. "Tell me more about that, Amir."

He paused, searching for the right words. "You know, when I started freelancing, I thought I'd find my groove," he said. "But now, it's like I'm in this weird space where I can't quite figure out what's happening."

I nodded, encouraging him continue. "What's changed for you since the beginning?"

"That's the puzzle," he replied with a touch of frustration. "I can't quite put my finger on it. It's like a part of me is missing or hidden away."

And he told me his story.

Amir took the leap into freelancing a few years before with a clear purpose:to take full control of his career, free from external rules and limitations. He wanted to bring his unique vision to his work and unlock his potential. Initially, everything fell into place, his years of effort paid off as he built a strong reputation in his niche, leading to consistent demand for his services. But over time, the excitement faded. "Somehow, I've lost the ability to bring what I call the 'true me' to my work."

'What exactly is that 'true me'?' I asked.

'I wish I could explain,' Amir exhaled.

The disconnect between his original aspirations and his current reality left Amir puzzled. He gazed at his latest design, one that should have filled him with satisfaction, only to be met with a sense of emptiness. Where had the energy gone? How had he strayed from the path he had so eagerly embarked upon?

Many people I work with go through similar phases, feeling that they lose their sense of self and they are not *true* anymore. You'll meet some of them in this chapter and the rest of the book.

But what is that exactly—*true me*? What is this elusive component, the absence of which we feel so deeply, yet struggle to articulate?

The first part of the "Who am I?" formula: the invisible part

There's a notion from the world of psychology called 'self-concept,'[1] which describes the thoughts and ideas we hold about ourselves. This mental portrait is crafted from our life experiences, our beliefs, the things we value, and how we engage with others. It's like the lens through which we see ourselves and make sense of everything around us. This is our understanding of who we really are.

A self-concept answers the question, "What makes me, me?" It's what we infuse into our work. When it's in sync, we feel true to ourselves, or, to put it scientifically, we're in the *zone of authenticity*.

Scholars have defined authenticity as behaving according to what one considers to be one's true self.[2] In simple terms, authenticity means your inner self and how you act on the outside are in harmony.

Several research studies have shown that feeling truly authentic is strongly linked to being more engaged at work[3, 4], and you are more likely to find a deeper sense of fulfillment and purpose[5]. When that connection is out of balance, on the other hand, you might find yourself facing an authenticity gap—that is exactly what Amir's experience is about.

On Authenticity Gap

There is a true mental and emotional cost when our work doesn't line up with who we really are.[6] Studies back this up, saying it can be mentally and emotionally exhausting.

"I caught myself pretending to be an enthusiastic leader for several years now, and I'm doing it because how I truly feel could potentially undermine my team and ultimately my career," wrote Olga, the head of client services at a bank.

Keeping up an inauthentic front can take a toll, leading to stress, burnout, and a dip in our overall well-being. When we're not staying true to who we are, we often end up doing tasks and projects that don't gel with our values or interests. This can leave us feeling empty and unfulfilled because we're not contributing in ways that really mean something to us.

The bigger the gap gets between our inner selves and what we're doing at work, the more frustration starts to build up. Imagine it as a reservoir slowly filling, drop by drop, each time we suppress our true selves for work roles.

The buildup of this frustration isn't immediately obvious, but its impact is widespread. It weakens motivation, enthusiasm for tasks, and overall well-being. The longer we keep up this façade, the more it drains our energy, leaving us with less for the things that really matter to us. Over time, this reservoir might reach a breaking point. This mirrors Amir's situation.

Here's another aspect of the authenticity gap. "You know what I hate the most?" shared Annika, an independent financial consultant. "Having to fill my social media with content about my successful career and life. I have to continuously convey that I'm exceptional and that I lead a diverse and fulfilling life as a sought-after professional. I'm compelled to play the same game at conferences and networking events, and sometimes, it takes more energy than the work itself!"

WHAT'S NEXT?

Attempting to portray ourselves as an idealized, polished, and flawless version is another common behavior that doesn't truly align with who we are—and in the digital age, more and more of us are expected to play the game. In either scenario, our genuine self remains suppressed, locked away.

But who we really are? What exactly we are talking about? What is this true self part? Let's find it.

Reflection Point

Practice "Feedback"

In this exercise, I'm offering you a series of hypothetical situations. Formulate your answers based on how you would truly want them to be regardless of where you work and what you do. Don't limit yourself by your current job.

1. Complete the client feedback statement that would empower you tremendously:

   "I'm glad you were the one working with me because you are the person who ………"

2. Complete the colleague recommendation statement:

   "I highly recommend him/her because he/she is the person who ………"

3. Complete the feedback on your presentation:

   "Among all the speakers on this topic, you are the most ……."

4. Complete the feedback on your book if you once wrote one:

   "Among all the books on this topic, yours is the most ……."

5. Complete the team feedback statement:

   "No one else brings as much ...... to the work as you do!"

   Keep in mind, when you're coming up with your answers, to think about how you'd truly want them to be in any job scenario.

   Be sure to use the focus-unfocus-refocus strategy for effective reflection. This will help you get the highest quality answers.

   Let's take a look at Amir's responses:

1. *"... because you're someone who had un unlimited creativity and flipped my perception of the subject."*
2. *"... because Amir is a person who can see what doesn't exist yet, and thinks outside the box."*
3. *"...you're the one who's the most creative and shattering preconceived notions."*
4. *"... yours is the one that seriously messes with my mind, changes my perspective, and opens my peepers wide."*
5. *"... as much creative juju and good times into the grind as you do!"*

How to unpack the results:

Before we dive into your results, keep in mind that this book uses 'thought-provoking' or 'exploratory' questions. These are meant to help you learn more about yourself and see things from new angles. There are no right or wrong answers. Your responses are unique to you and reveal different aspects of your identity.

For those who are detail-oriented, you might be tempted to delve into the minutiae of each response. However, it's vital to avoid getting lost in over-analysis. The objective is not to find exhaustive or perfect answers or concrete, definitive conclusions, but rather to open up new avenues of thought and self-understanding.

Now, let's look at what you have. Your answers reflect how you currently see yourself. Remember that this part of us changes throughout our lives. So, what we're seeing now is just a snapshot of this stage.

What picture of yourself comes out from your answers?

I asked Amir what he sees. "Looking at these responses, I must be some kind of super unorthodox, idea-shooting creative dude," Amir quipped. "But you know, I like it! I see all the stuff I truly dig, and it's all pretty darn me" he added.

Now it's your turn—what self-concept do you extract from your answers? Give yourself the opportunity to reflect.

How to Use This Newfound Understanding?

First of all, our self-concept, or our true self, doesn't take the form of a job title or a profession; it's what we infuse into every work we undertake.

Take a group of schoolteachers, for example. They all have the same job title, but if they're being authentic, you'll see their individuality shine through. One might be super supportive, another might be all about structure and organization. One could be known for their humor and charisma, another might have a real passion for science, and the last one might stand out for their discipline and precision.

What really sets them apart isn't the profession itself, but the way they've integrated their own personality and style into their day-to-day.

"I never thought about it like that," said Amir. "So, does that mean a job is just like a mould? And no matter what I am—a designer, a professor, or a help desk specialist—I'll be a mega-creative, unorthodox version of that?"

Right.

Now, take some time to think about this and try to recall how your self-concept shows up in your work and life.

This sense of who you truly are, regardless of where you work, is the first part of the "Who am I" equation. Let's move on to the second part, and it's going to get even more intriguing from here!

The second part of the "Who am I?" formula: the visible part

This part of your 'Who am I' formula is what others can see, probably what's listed on your LinkedIn page, like your job title and role. Designer. HR Director. Finance Manager. Founder. Career strategist.

Since a role represents the visible aspect of ourselves, it's often what we focus on when we ask 'who am I?' This question kind of takes us back to a childhood one: 'What will I become when I grow up?'

I often hear from mid-career professionals that they still haven't found an answer to this question, even though they've been trying to figure it out their whole lives. Recently, I had a session with Laura, a 37-year-old project manager. She confessed that she's envious of people who know exactly who they are and have found fulfilment in their jobs. She's still searching for that kind of clarity, despite putting in a lot of effort to find her answers and define who she is.

She's not alone. Even Amir, who had seemingly found his answer as a graphic designer, questions the validity of it. He's doubting whether it's the right answer, as it doesn't bring him satisfaction or a sense of fulfilling his potential. "What if I'm not meant to be a graphic designer at all? Maybe I should be a street musician or an artist instead? Sometimes I feel like I'm something more than just a graphic designer," he said as we delved into the second part of the formula.

Why is it so hard to define ourselves by our roles?

Perhaps it's because there's something fundamentally flawed in the way we go about it.

What does the old traditional model prescribe when it comes to discovering 'Who am I'? It should be: *one right answer; found as early as possible; defined once and for all.*

And this is where the problems begin.

WHAT'S NEXT?

Have you ever heard of "identity foreclosure"? It's used to describe a scenario where someone decide on a certain profession too soon, without really seeing what else is out there. When people rush into this kind of decision, it might lead to issues down the road. This can leave them feeling lost, unhappy, or like they've missed out on other opportunities.

Take Sarah, for example. From a young age, she was told that she should strive for success and financial stability. Her parents, both successful accountants, had their hearts set on her joining a prestigious Big 4 accounting firm. Sarah's childhood was filled with stories of their achievements and how their hard work had paved the way for a comfortable life.

As Sarah got older, her parents' expectations became more pronounced. They pictured her walking in their shoes, decked out in business suits, and handling boardroom meetings. To them, making it big in the Big 4 was the ultimate success, and they were set on Sarah going down that road. But now, after nine years in the field, she's hit a realization: she never chose this path for herself.

Here's Alex, a chemist whose life's trajectory was influenced by one high school teacher in particular. His chemistry teacher recognized his aptitude for science and encouraged him to pursue a career in the field. With unwavering enthusiasm, the teacher guided Alex down a path she believed would guarantee success—a journey into the world of pharmaceuticals and research.

WHAT'S NEXT?

With his teacher's approval and his family's expectations weighing on him, Alex started college as a chemistry major—it felt like the obvious choice. But as he got deeper into his studies, he began to wonder if this path matched his innermost dreams.

So, why does this tradition persist? It's not just because parents always ask the question, "What do you want to be when you grow up?" It's also because the educational system in many countries often focuses on early specializations and selecting majors early on, which creates a lot of expectations around getting them "right."

I was doing a radio interview once, and people were calling in with questions about careers and finding their way. One woman sounded really concerned. She wanted advice for her son, who was struggling to figure out what profession he should pursue. She felt anxious because he was spending a lot of time pondering this question. When I asked how old her son was, she said he's twelve. Twelve years old, I thought. How could he possibly know at that age? I could just imagine all the pressure and expectations on that boy. It's surprising how these outdated approaches still hang around.

Luckily, there are exceptions. One couple I know don't pester their teenage daughter with the usual question. Instead, they use an exploratory approach. When she shares future aspirations, her parents help her to arrange experiences related to those professions—internship, short training, shadowing. Their aim is to keep her from getting fixated on a single idea of herself too early, steering clear of the danger of narrowing her perspective before she even starts her professional journey. They have a simple rationale: they want to ensure she doesn't develop tunnel vision.

Tunnel vision is the main trap that comes from aiming to pinpoint your one true professional identity too early in the game.

But if the old model is broken, what instead?

In fact, this journey of discovery into who you are is more interesting than you might think and I invite you to explore it. First, though, fasten your seatbelts, because you'll never anticipate what's coming next.

You Are More Than One Thing

The good news is that you don't have to chain yourself to the one and only professional identity or role—by design, we are a portfolio of them. According to modern identity theories, we are a multitude of possible selves.[9]

We're much more than just one thing, even in a single career or under one job title. Consider my client whom I'll call Maria, a Brand Manager at a digital media agency. She acts as a Brand Specialist, ensuring that all marketing efforts align with the company's brand identity; a Leader for his team; a Mentor to junior colleagues, providing guidance and expertise; a Trend Spotter and Innovator, always on the lookout for new technologies to introduce to her company; an Author, who writes for industry journals; and a Consultant, offering her expertise to charities to boost their digital presence.

Our identities showcase our key professional facets and and mix together in different ways as we go through our careers. Some are prominent and well-defined, while others are more subtle, supporting us in the background. For Maria, recent additions to her identity include being an Author and a Consultant. Meanwhile, some roles like Administrator or Content Writer, which marked the start of her career, no longer fit her current trajectory. Other identities are still forming, shaped by our ongoing experiences. Just three years ago, Maria wasn't interested in mentoring or teaching, yet today, these roles energize her immensely.

If you take me, for example, I'm now a Writer, but I also have a strong identity as a Mentor, and a very important identity as a subject matter Expert. Apart from all of these, I have a Researcher inside. And last but not least, I am a Teacher and Educator. Sometimes I vividly see a picture of all my inner professionals as a group portrait—the Researcher has Einstein's mustache, the Writer sits at a 100-year-old typewriter (which exists in reality, in my study)—everyone represents one of my key professional role or facets.

In portfolio careers, the mix can be particularly fascinating. My husband Roman works as a General Manager by day, and in his spare time, he runs a "garage" project as a hi-fi Designer, where he crafts and sells custom-designed speakers.

Even if someone has just one job title, they can still have different sides to them. An HR Director, for instance, isn't just a single identity. Take my friend Ann, for example: she is also a Boss for their subordinates, and an Advisor whose words echo in the boardroom, and even a Thought Leader, penning insights for business magazines on human development.

In my lectures, I frequently notice a collective sigh of relief when I encourage professionals to wholeheartedly embrace their diverse, and at times, divergent identities. It's as if a burden is lifted because many people instinctively feel that they're not just a single identity. Embracing this realization can ease stress and, with time, allow the numerous layers of their authentic selves to shine through.

Study shows that fitting within the bounds of a single work identity may require suppressing important parts of oneself[10, 11]. Letting go of the idea that there's only one "right" professional identity can lift a ton of pressure. Realizing that there are many potential answers to "Who am I professionally?" eases our worries about making the wrong choice. This makes our career journey more about discovery and enjoyment, rather than stress and doubt.

Reflection point

Uncovering your multiple identities

Let's keep delving into your journey, and now we're moving on to the second phase of exploration. In the glow of all that's been shared, we're reshaping the question "Who am I?" into a fresh and far more intriguing: "*What am I made of?*"

1. What are you made of? Create a list of all your identities and inner professionals that reside within you.

I already gave my example; now it's Amir's turn. After taking a time to contemplate, he wrote me, that "in his designer guise, he stumbled upon three distinct personas: the diligent Designer of design tasks, the rebellious Artist brimming with wild ideas, and the Nerd, who likes to dig deeper into the subject."

"At first, I thought, wow, this isn't just splitting personality, it's like identity scramble! But truthfully, I've always suspected I couldn't be crammed into just one thing. A part of me will always be hanging out," he exclaimed when we met.

2. How do you act out your identities now? Which of them are in focus?

Is something missed or underrepresented?

In recent years, Amir hasn't been releasing his Artist into the world much and has hardly given a voice to his inner Nerd. "My inner Designer was busy tackling orders to make ends meet in freelancing, but he's just a part of me, and certainly not the most invigorating," Amir remarked. "It's no wonder I found myself adrift within my profession!"

"When was the last time your artistic side came out?" I asked.

"Hmm, that's a great question. Seems like I haven't embraced it in years."

That totally makes sense, and scholars also emphasize that the crucial element in building your identity is "enactment." Enactment is like the fuel that keeps the identity engine running. If identity is the response to the question "Who am I?" then the answer is "I am who I enact."[12]

3. In what combination do you want them to be in the next stage? Which identity (identities) do you desire to showcase more prominently?

A few years ago, I made a decision to be more of an Expert than a Manager and to set loose my inner Researcher, who had never found enough time in my schedule.

Amir made up his mind that the identity he desired most, yet had neglected, was that of an Artist. "I definitely want to focus on my creativity in the next phase. I sense there's a reservoir of energy waiting for me there," he said.

"All that's left is to figure out how I ended up losing it," he added.

True Self, False Self: How Do We Accidentally Lose Who We Are?

"To be nobody but yourself in a world which is doing its best day and night to make you like everybody else means to fight the hardest battle which any human being can fight and never stop fighting."—E.E. Cummings

I have an idea of who might have the answer to Amir's question. D.W. Winnicott was a British psychoanalyst and an author of theory of True and False selves. He posits that in childhood we learned to comply in order to be loved, and we had to follow social norms and other people's expectations in order to be accepted and recognised.[13]

Adult professionals frequently find themselves on a similar journey. In their pursuit of impressive accomplishments, meeting client and stakeholder demands, and achieving financial goals, they can gradually become detached from their authentic selves.

Let's go back to Amir. At the start, when he began freelancing, it was really exciting. He could pick the work he wanted, make his own schedule, and follow his creative instincts. But over time, things started to change bit by bit. The pure joy of being creative began to mix with the need to earn money and build a stable career.

Amir came to the realisation that he was accepting projects not only driven by his creative passion, but also based on what clients were willing to compensate him for. The fine balance between his creativity and his income had shifted, and he discovered that he was giving precedence to the commercial viability of his work over the initial spark that had ignited his passion.

But it's never too late to rekindle that connection and align your work with who you are.

When Amir acknowledged that his true creative self is lost in the pursuit of tangible results, he took time to rethink how his inner Artist showed up in his projects. He decided to change the criteria for accepting incoming projects and accept them only if there is room for creativity. Besides, he joined a community of creative designers.

"Isn't it funny? I've always wanted to be part of this crew, but never found the time," he mused. "Those folks are up to some seriously wild ventures. There's so much to soak in!" Listening to this, I was delighted by the energy in his words. That's why I believe those 'what's next?' moments are so important. Even if they are tough, they help us understand who we are, tap into our full potential, and align our career path with it.

Remember, Who You Are Is Up to You to Decide

"I live as if my real story hasn't even started yet," said Lucy, a single mother of two, who works as an administrator in a clinic. Her job provides her with the necessary financial stability, but, as she puts it, "It's absolutely not who I am."

Beyond her conventional job, Lucy dedicates almost every evening to crafting artisanal chocolates, often made to order. On weekends, she conducts chocolate masterclasses. She invested in a high-quality professional chocolate-making course a few years ago, even taking out a bank loan to cover it. She handed me a

WHAT'S NEXT?

box of her homemade chocolates when we first met, and the flavor still lingers in my memory.

"I'm unsure if I can make a real living as a chocolatier and leave my day job; it's like I'm in some kind of deadlock," she shared, her voice tinged with sadness.

As I held the box of her exquisite chocolates—undeniably real—in my hand, I imagined the hours she poured into her "second job." A question naturally arose.

I asked her: "Lucy, is your story about being a chocolatier with a daytime administrator's role, or is it about being an administrator who has a chocolate hobby?"

She paused to process my question, and goosebumps crept up my skin as she gave me a different look.

After a pause, she shared that her life's narrative seemed to undergo a reset in her mind. Her passion for chocolate now took the spotlight as the central theme. "I've been accustomed to repeating that someday I'll become a chocolatier. But... I'm already living it now!"

I have seen this magic many times: as soon as we realize that we are the ones who define what our story is about, we stop living as if it were decided for us. We stop feeling that something is missing and our real story has not even started.

In fact, it might have started years ago.

Who you are, that's only up to you to decide.

Key Points

Answering the question "Who am I?" involves delving into two crucial aspects:

- Your self-concept: What kind of person are you when you are being your true and authentic self?

  This is your personal understanding of what makes you uniquely you, and it serves as the driving force behind your work, extending beyond your job title. This is who you are if you are not this job title anymore.

- Your multiple roles: You're not limited to a single professional identity; you're a mosaic of roles, each reflecting a different aspect of you. The key is to decide in what combination you want these roles to be in the next stage of your life.

Give yourself enough time to stay with this question before moving on to others. Remember the incubation stage—live with your answers and allow new insights to come from within. I hope you enjoyed the process we've gone through.

Chapter 2. "What Is My Passion?"

"I am totally sure that marketing is not my passion anymore," said Lisa, the disengaged marketing executive who you met in the very first paragraph of this book. "Was it ever? " she contemplated, stirring her coffee.

"Now, I want something new that will make me happy, something I'll enjoy for the rest of my career," she added.

Passion is one of the most frequently encountered words in the requests that come in to me: *'the passion has gone', 'help me find what makes me tick', 'help me find what makes me come alive'.*

"I haven't the faintest clue what that might be; all I know is that it must not be marketing," Lisa continued. "But what exactly? I've considered all the important questions, from imagining my life five years from now to describing my perfect day. But none of it seems to bring me clarity, you know."

Have you ever spent some time delving into the kinds of questions that are supposed to shine a spotlight on your passion? Let's start from there.

Top Five Perplexing 'Find-Your-Passion' Questions

It's no surprise that these questions often fall short—some of the most common ones are more confusing than enlightening. Lisa is not alone in her struggle, and since these questions are pervasive, let me explain why they might not provide the answers you seek. Here they are:

1. "Describe your ideal day."
2. "Where do you see yourself five to 10 years from now?"
3. "If you had five lives, what would you do in each of them?"
4. "What would you do if you only had six months/ three months/ one month to live?"
5. "If money was not an issue at all, what would you be doing with your life?"

Let's examine each of them closely.

1. "Describe your ideal day."

The intended aim of this question is to help you visualize an inspiring scenario and gain insights into your career aspirations and passion.

However, what often happens is that most of us create an image that is a stark contrast to our current life. The more exhausted we are, the more extreme and idealistic our vision becomes. This can lead to frustration because the ideal future seems so far and unattainable. Additionally, people tend to focus on personal life rather than work, imagining a day spent in a beautiful coastal house with a relaxing morning routine, filled with activities they enjoy with loved ones. This doesn't provide much professional insight.

2. "Where do you see yourself five to 10 years from now?"

The intended aim of this question is to help you identify your long-term professional goal and provide a sense of direction.

But in practice, this question generates more frustration than any other, because it implies that you already should know The One and Only Right Answer about your future. If you are not certain, like a lot of us, you could think, "What's wrong with me? I am 30 (35, 40, etc.) and I still don't know who I want to be once I grow up... "

3. "If you had five lives, what would you do in each of them?"

The aim of this question: to give you a list of work that feels like you and, as a result, gives you a possible direction.

Paradoxically, mid-careers often perceive it as a list of dreams that will never be fulfilled rather than a list of inspiring ideas. And instead of provoking light-bulb moments, it might provide you with more "it's-too-late" feelings than before. It's too late to become a doctor, a scientist, a sports champion, etc.

4. "What would you do if you only had six months/ three months/ one month to live?"

The intended aim of this question is to uncover your deep interests and true passions—what you would pursue even if you knew your time was limited.

In practice, this question is not helpful for determining long-term professional priorities. Instead, it often leads to reflections on life priorities such as spending time with loved ones or fulfilling personal experiences. It doesn't typically generate strategic career goals like becoming a professional in a specific field, starting a business, or developing specific job-related skills, as the limited time frame doesn't allow for long-term planning.

5. "If money was not an issue at all, what would you be doing with your life?"

The intended aim of this question is to explore your true interests free from financial constraints, encouraging you to make choices from the heart.

In practice, alas, it rarely focuses on professional interests. If you ask me (by the way, I love my job!), I'd say that I would travel all the time and, in between trips, watch BBC's "Fake or Fortune" and sports docuseries. As many mid-career people already feel drained, if money were not an issue, they might prioritize rest and relaxation over taking on new professional challenges. This question may not uncover career-related passions.

All of these questions share a fundamental flaw—they rely on a risky approach, expecting you to sit down and excavate new answers from your mind, all while working with the same set of data. But you'll never discover your passion for becoming a captain if you've never seen the sea.

You Can't Be What You Can't See

"Trying to squeeze new ideas out of my brain, that's what I did many times." Lisa smiled. "But there is nothing new in it, no ideas, no options."

"Not a surprise for me," I said to Lisa, "Busy achievers living in a space of their current job, and if they have families, they have even less time to look around."

There may be a lot of interesting things around us, right nearby, that haven't yet appeared on our radars. My friend Amy had never thought about health and wellness as a career path until she went to see a nutritionist. My current role as an independent career strategist was entirely off my radar, too, although it's closely related to my previous position as a corporate talent specialist.

Take a glance at some of the comments on my social media where people share their experiences of discovering something when they venture beyond their habitat.

"I recently read about a new profession called 'digital linguist.' It involves incorporating artificial intelligence into people's lives and developing algorithms for AI-human interaction. I work in IT myself, and languages are my hobby! I never thought of how they could connect, so I was surprised and inspired by that!"

"At your lecture, I met a woman who works in art marketing. It opened up a wonderful new world of cultural projects, galleries, and exquisite events for me. I almost thought marketing wasn't for me..."

"I enjoy simplifying complexity through clear text structures, visualization, and the right words. The first time I discovered it when I saw a presentation by an advertising agency. I knew I wanted that too. Now I'm a presentation scriptwriter."

"After two years of studying to become a stylist, I started practicing, but I was struggling to find my niche. That's when I made a decision to watch videos from 20 different stylists on YouTube, from various fields. Surprisingly, very few of them resonated with me—except for a jewelry stylist. As I watched her videos, it became clear that this was the path I wanted to pursue. She even guided me on where to further my studies. And now, I'm proud to say, I've become a jewelry stylist."

As you can see, these people had no clue which information would impact them at a pivotal moment. These options couldn't be guessed or invented thorough contemplation—they were nowhere in their minds.

After many years of practice, I've come to a conclusion: we feel stuck and fail to see opportunities not because they don't exist, but because we can't spot them from where we are at the moment.

Finding Your Passion: Light-Bulb Moments

Lisa started her rediscovery process by meeting new people and going to new places. Two weeks into her exploration, she messaged me with excitement, saying, "Lena, you won't believe it! One of my classmates is a dog psychologist. I've always loved animals, and I think this might be the path for me!"

Wow! A light-bulb moment! You might assume that this is the happy moment in Lisa's search that led her to her true passion, but it's not. However, it is a good moment for us to learn something important: those light-bulb moments don't always guarantee that it's the right answer.

Since this is one of the strongest myths associated with finding your passion, I would like to delve into it in more detail.

Once, I invited members of my audience who seemed truly happy in their work to share their stories about discovering their passion.

One woman, who started as a corporate manager but eventually became a creator of her own clothing brand, described feeling rejuvenated and inspired after meandering through a fabric store and later crafting something by hand. Then, one day, while going through her childhood diary, she stumbled upon a section titled, "What do you want to be when you grow up?" In that section, she found a clear and vivid declaration, written in her own young handwriting: "Fashion Designer"... BOOM! It struck her like lightning!

Another woman shared her experience: "I once opened a job listings magazine in a completely different field – it was a guide for gastronomic tours. It was like a bolt of lightning, hitting me with a powerful realisation: combining the city, gastronomy, storytelling, and guiding people – could anything be more fascinating?" This woman, who had been a university lecturer, is now working as a tour guide.

Similarly, a former manager turned hi-fi designer recounted, "I was in the midst of assembling a home audio system and, to my surprise, found myself very excited as I explored the intricate nuances of sound. I eagerly anticipated the end of the workday just so I could dive back into this captivating subject. Even though I had already purchased and installed the system, I couldn't resist immersing myself further. A few years later, I launched my own production venture in my garage."

There were numerous responses, and one reader even went a step further by analyzing these stories and creating a roadmap: first, there's a sense of sadness and longing, then the moment of discovering one's passion with a brilliant realization. Afterward, decisions are made, leading to eventual success.

This is how many of us perceive passion, isn't it? As an explosion of emotions, an uplifting mood, inspiration, and flow. Scholars define the feeling of passion as a strong inclination toward an activity that people genuinely enjoy, consider significant, and invest their time and energy into[1]. Passion is characterized by intense positive emotions[2] and provides the psychological energy necessary for pursuing it[3]. Therefore, it's no surprise that we expect our emotions to send us a strong signal when we've found our true passion. Does it really work like this?

My little experiment didn't conclude there. A week later, I asked my audience to share different stories. This time, I was particularly interested in situations where people initially felt a resounding "this is it!" and had an emotional explosion of excitement, only to discover later that this wasn't the answer they were looking for. Here's what I found in the comments:

A sales professional wrote, "I approached photography with enthusiasm, delving into camera settings and its capabilities. I took courses and even attended a photography school, and it all seemed perfect. I could teach people photography! But... I quickly realized that explaining camera settings to others and critiquing their photos and mistakes wasn't my forte."

A product manager shared, "I attempted to become a public speaking consultant. Initially, I felt the spark, even more so since I've always loved public speaking myself. Then, I started studying the theory. However, I soon became disinterested; I was missing the 'product' and the business aspect of it."

"I yearned for something more creative and inspiring," a marketing research specialist wrote, "I admired two acquaintances who were florists, content with their lives and careers. I envisioned the joy of arranging bouquets all day, every day, not just occasionally. So, I decided to study it. I obtained a diploma and derived immense satisfaction, but I also suffered from excruciating back pain and severe burns from the glue gun. I realized I could never make a living from this."

"I had an epiphany—I wanted to become a food photographer!" said a finance manager. "I began studying it. However, I quickly discovered that food photography demands meticulous, almost tedious framing down to the millimeter and

1000 attempts for each shot. Sounds even more boring that my current job."

"Oh, how I dreamed of an eco farm: goats, wine... I read everything, planned it all. I even quit my job. Thank goodness I didn't buy a farm but started volunteering first. After a month of milking and goat mastitis, followed by another month of agricultural toil in 40-degree heat on a 45-degree slope, I came to terms with the fact that farm life was nothing like what I had envisioned," recounted a software quality assurance team leader.

An 'a-ha' moment and a profound insight might seem like strong signals that you've found your right answer. However, in the end, all of that are just assumptions and hypotheses.

Light bulb moments are just assumptions.

I suggested to Lisa that she find a way to test her idea about becoming a dog psychologist. She decided to shadow her classmate for a few days at work. A week later she returned with doubts. "I love dogs, but this work is not really about them; it's more about dog owners, which isn't as interesting," she explained. "I think my classmate's passion was more contagious for me than my own interest in her field. So, I don't believe this is my calling, but at least I helped her with her marketing," she added with a smile. I often see this 'contagious effect' among those who are desperately looking for a passion.

Lisa was feeling a bit disappointed, and I understand why. It had been a few weeks of searching for her passion, and she hadn't found anything yet. Like any true achiever, she wanted results as quickly as possible.

"If only I had a dream!" she exclaimed. "It would make things so much easier now! My friend, for example, is certain that one day she'll open her coffee shop in Tenerife! Why don't I have something like that?" She shook her head in disappointment.

I quickly reassured Lisa that it wasn't as clear-cut as it seemed, and that dreams are essentially, well, just hypotheses.

Dreams, on Closer Examination

A few years ago, I met a couple who had recently sold their family restaurant in a small port town on the French Riviera. The chef, Alexander, had owned the cozy restaurant for three years, but for the previous seven years, he had dreamt of it while working as a bank clerk in a big city.

"I knew there would be a different life. There's the sea, it's beautiful. I'd be able to cook, which I adore. I envisioned something real, connected with people, not just with papers and numbers. A was dreaming about loyal clients and the opportunity to bring them joy."

Then, one day, Alexander's dream became a reality, but not quite as he had imagined. He discovered that the love for cooking can quickly wane when you're hustling in a cramped, sweltering kitchen, constantly crunching numbers to ensure there's enough to cover next month's taxes. The idyllic images of a slow-paced life in a stunning locale remained confined to his imagination, while he found himself spending even less time with his children than before. Financial constraints led his wife to step in as a waitress because hiring additional staff was costly. And after a few months, he realized he had made a mistake.

When this happens, it's understandably disappointing, but believe it or not, dreams don't always reflect what you really want.

Over time, I noticed an interesting pattern: the dreams of exhausted professionals often share a common trait: they stand in stark contrast to the person's current job reality.

I've observed five distinct types of these contrasting, or escape, dreams:

1. Contrasting Picture

Imagine this: a vast savannah, a person with a camera capturing a mesmerizing sunset. That's what my dream of becoming a travel photographer looked like. Dreams such as these often revolve around atmospheric coffee shops, scuba diving on tropical islands, artist studios, peaceful yoga classes, hikes to breathtaking viewpoints, pottery workshops, seaside restaurants, and hotels nestled in picturesque forests. They are vibrant, colorful, and filled with sunshine – a stark departure from the usual working routines.

2. Contrasting Meaning

In the realm of traditional corporate roles, the idea of transitioning into being a coach, trainer, psychologist, rescuer, educator, stylist, or another helping profession presents a stark contrast to the reality of being a mere cog in a massive machine, seldom receiving recognition.

3. Contrasts in Creativity

The more a job feels dull, repetitive, and governed by algorithms, the more a person yearns for creativity — the act of bringing something new into existence. This could be dreams about painting, photography, crafting jewelry or clothing, designing, decorating interiors, arranging bouquets, or writing poetry or prose.

4. Contrasts in Results

Have you ever wondered why seasoned professionals often dream of engaging in something simple like baking bread, cooking, crafting ceramic pots, grooming dogs, or brewing coffee in a cafe? These dreams share a common thread — a short distance to a sense of accomplishment. It's when your invested energy comes back to you. This completes a cycle that frequently remains unfinished in our regular jobs. Therefore, someone working on a year-and-a-half-long project dreams of baking bread, driven not only by their love for baking but mainly by their yearning for tangible results.

5. Contrasts in Freedom

No bosses. No set schedules or timetables. Working for oneself. Absolute freedom. Perhaps today, some of you once again contemplated how exasperating your boss can be and how liberating it would be without them. It's a natural thought.

However, in the early years of my practice, I was surprised to discover that half of my unfulfilled clients were individuals who were already their own bosses. But reality is more intricate and fulfillment doesn't merely revolve around the absence of a boss.

At times, the dreams of weary professionals encompass all these contrasts, and sometimes they focus on just one. So, what should you do? Should you stop dreaming? Fear your ideas? Underestimate them?

Absolutely not. First, interpret these dreams as manifestations of something important currently missing, think about what message they convey and what meaning lies behind them. Second, harness them for the good.

Dreams: A Sort of User Manual

Dreams can lead you in the wrong direction only if you disregard the key rule of safety. Yes, believe it or not, there are rules, and they are based on the lessons learned from mistakes and regrets.

The primary error lies in harboring a dream for an extended period, making the monumental decision to abandon everything, burning your bridges, and embarking on its pursuit without any prior exploration. Alexander, who dreamed of owning a restaurant for a long time and went all-in on it, followed this pattern.

A dream, even one that has lingered with you for a decade, remains nothing more than a hypothesis until it's put to the test. This is the main rule of safety.

In the "just go for it!" approach, the saddest outcome is realizing that you've ended up in the wrong place, leading to disappointment in yourself and a reluctance to pursue change in the future. On the other hand, in the "do nothing" approach, there's even less that's good. It's also a losing option.

So, what's the winning strategy? How to go about dreams?

My answer is: try them out! Approach them. Experience them. Test them.

To test a dream, such as owning a restaurant, you don't have to dive in headfirst with lots of planning and debt. Instead, you can dip your toes in by working at a restaurant during your next vacation. It might lead to something new or just be a fun experience. Both outcomes are great.

You see, every dream, whether it turns out to be a mirage or a dream worth pursuing, contains a substantial reservoir of energy. *A dream is energy*, and it's nothing good when it remains trapped within the confines of a closed space. From there, it begins to emit signals, reminding you of its existence and fostering a sense that something crucial has been missed in your life. However, when you comprehend your dreams and learn to derive positive experiences from them in the present, you'll acquire many benefits.

Chasing your dreams changes how you feel. It's like turning up the brightness in your life. You get more energy, determination, and motivation to achieve things. With these, you can accomplish a lot. Feeling happy and excited isn't something you only get when you succeed; it's more like a fuel that helps you succeed.

Also, chasing your dreams helps you learn more about yourself. It's like exploring new parts of who you are, enacting your new identities. In the previous chapter, we discussed that not all of your professional selves may have had the chance to emerge into the light, this will happen through trying yourself in new roles and new topics.

But, above all, pursuing your dreams brings you a profound sense of contentment and fulfillment. You don't have to fit all your interests and talents into just one thing. You can have multiple careers or interests, and you can pursue them alongside your current job. Right now, people like you are doing all sorts of things—like taking singing lessons, helping out at hospitals and events, learning to bake bread, acting in community theater, starting their own podcasts or YouTube channels, writing poems, or making clothes.

The most important thing about all of this is that you feel like you're not missing out on anything in life. You're not putting things off for some vague "someday" in the future. You're living for today.

Now, let's return to Lisa. She felt better when she realized that simply having a ready-to-use dream doesn't guarantee that everything will magically fall into place. When I mentioned escape dreams, she told me she recognized in herself this strong feeling of searching for a new passion as far away from marketing as possible.

I assured her that it's a common instinct to search as far as possible from home. But why does it happen?

On the Instinct to Search for New Passion Far Away from Home

The first reason is the desire for change. Burnout and career crises can lead to a strong urge for a new start, pushing us to seek opportunities far beyond our current settings. The more drastic the change, the more refreshing it can seem.

Another reason is escaping from our overwhelming current situations. When we're struggling in our jobs, we often fantasize about living completely different lives. We might long to escape to new places where the problems of our current jobs just don't exist.

A third element is reinvention. Distance from familiar settings can feel like a blank slate—a chance to reinvent oneself without the baggage of past failures or frustrations. New places can feel like they offer new beginnings and new versions of ourselves.

Additionally, there's the romanticization of the unknown. During periods of dissatisfaction, there's a tendency to view new places or radically different careers as inherently better than one's current situation. This perspective can make the grass seem greener elsewhere.

Finally, psychological relief plays a role. Stepping away from the known environment reduces immediate stress and provides psychological relief. The distance allows us to detach from current stresses and potentially view our situation from a new perspective.

It's crucial to grasp these dynamics; they can lead us to make choices driven more by the urge to escape than by thoughtful planning. This blinds us to the value of our current field and causes us to overlook good opportunities right in front of us.

So, I suggested that this time, Lisa should start exploring from where she is now, so she doesn't miss any good opportunities. I told her that people often find their new passion near the place where they lost the old one and reminded her of my own example. When we started our big transition in 2011, I could imagine various career paths for myself, but not the one I was in at the time. Why? Because I was already in this industry, and I was unhappy! Back then, I didn't even know that a job like an independent career strategist existed. I never thought of seeking the answer so close to my then field—talent development. I had cognitive blindness – I was absolutely certain that I had to look for something completely different from everything I had done before. If someone had shown me any picture from the future – perhaps from a career change seminar or the cover of my book – it would have shocked me. I firmly believed back then that what I was seeking was entirely different, and this belief was unshakable.

Now I understand that I didn't lose interest in the professional topic itself, but rather in the format in which I was operating at the time. The topic was talent and career development, and the format was corporate talent specialist. I equated them – if I didn't like being a corporate talent specialist, then I must not be interested in the topic of career development. The logic wasn't great, but who in a state of burnout analyzes things rationally?

So, it makes a lot of sense to rediscover your current field first and explore related industries. And I have an idea of how to do this in the quickest way.

3x3x3 Tool

Here's a simple tool I suggest for exploring possibilities within a specific industries and areas of interest. I call it the 3x3x3 tool.

First, find *three books* that have been published on this topic in the past year. These books can provide insights from experts in the field and offer information on the latest trends and tools.

Next, identify *three events* that are happening or have happened this year related to your chosen industry. These could be conferences, forums, or exhibitions. These events bring together people from different areas within the field and can give you a sense of current issues and actual niches.

Lastly, pinpoint *three individuals* who have achieved success in this field. Learning from people who are already successful in the area you're interested in can be incredibly valuable. Role models can provide inspiration and guidance as you explore your chosen topic. They are like treasure troves of information. Their experiences, educational paths, and involvement in professional communities—all of it is valuable.

Lisa continued her exploration journey, this time sticking much closer to her professional domain—marketing. During one of the conferences, she encountered an evangelist's presentation. An evangelist, as she explained, is someone who possesses the unique skill of championing cutting-edge technological products.

"I was utterly astounded that such a profession even existed," Lisa exclaimed. "If it hadn't, I might have had to invent it! I'm keen to invite this woman for a virtual coffee chat on Zoom and talk about her experiences and the path she's trodden. But based on what I've already gathered, my background in marketing seems like the ideal springboard for this!"

A week later, Lisa reached out again, reporting that the Zoom coffee meetup had taken place, and she'd connected with a small but intriguing professional community.

Lisa's journey of exploration went on, and evangelism seemed like a remarkably strong hypothesis. Some time later, we met in Paris, in the Luxembourg Gardens. We found a spot near the central pond and then continued our conversation as we strolled along the alleys.

The question she asked me in the end of our meeting there was very much expected:

"How do I make sure this is the one I'll enjoy for the rest of my career?" she asked.

I believe that sooner or later you'll ask yourself the same question. I know this because driven achievers aim to invest their time strategically, always with an eye on the long-term game.

It's time to share with you and Lisa two critical truths about your passion.

Truth #1: It's Not for the Rest of Your Career

We can't do the same things all the time and feel the same level of excitement. There is a part of our brain that always craves exploration, learning and something new.[5] Neuroscientists call it *the seeking system*. This system motivates us to explore. It's linked to the release of dopamine, a neurotransmitter associated with pleasure and reward.[6]

"What will I always enjoy doing?" is a question based on the false assumption that if we can maintain the same level of excitement forever. Even in your dream job you'll inevitably want something new to stay engaged and inspired.

I've spent many years focusing on career strategy and hope to continue for much longer. I'm confident it will always excite me, as I no longer expect to do the same things within this field all the time. I know how to keep it interesting for myself by learning new aspects of the topic, practicing different activities, and reinventing my work whenever I want.

I arrived at this approach not because I'm exceptionally wise or a genius, but rather because my job has led me to this realisation, as well as the next one.

Truth #2: It's Not Just About "What," But Also "How"

The "follow your passion" self-help industry tends to under-emphasize this key point: "Once you find your passion, everything will fall into place". It's almost a canonized idea, but in reality it's not that simple.

Joy and energy we extract from our interest depends not on the subject itself. Pack the same interest in different context and you will see the different result.

Let's take writing. Writing is my passion, but it wouldn't be if I had to write about boring topics, for people I don't like, or under tight deadlines. The subject of our interest isn't everything, even though we often think it is. What really matters is the context and the variables at play. These variables include where you work, the tasks you handle, your clients, the quality of your colleagues and supervisors, your schedule, your level of autonomy, and much more.

"Are you saying that I might hate being an evangelist if I work in a toxic environment? Or with a toxic boss? Or perhaps if I'm not truly engaged with the product I'm promoting?" asked Lisa.

"And vice versa, you may rekindle your passion for it if you land in the right context and have nothing to spoil it for you," I remarked. Lisa slowed down and fell into thought. We reached the exit of Luxembourg Gardens and said our goodbyes. Let's leave Lisa for a while with her reflections; we'll meet her again later in this book, as well as this 'how' aspect. I have more to share about it.

Interlude: Is Passion Found or Developed?

As we wrap up this chapter dedicated to the "What is my passion?" question, I want to share one more crucial insight. We've been circling the idea of *finding* passion, but it's not the only way to obtain it. Historically, two schools of thought have emerged on this matter.

First, there's the belief that passion is a fixed entity, either existing externally or deep within us, waiting to be uncovered. According to this perspective, all we need to do is locate it.

Second, there's the notion that passion and calling aren't predetermined but rather evolve through exploration and cultivation.

The first approach is a familiar one: the idea of a calling being akin to love at first sight, a lifelong passion lying in wait for our discovery. Numerous books and success stories have extolled this concept. We are encouraged to *find* our passion, pre-formed and merely in need of uncovering.

The second approach may not garner as much fanfare, but it is more scientifically grounded and gaining in popularity. Researchers have delved into the origins of passion, exploring where interests come from and how they develop. Are interests pre-existing, waiting for revelation, or must a spark of interest be nurtured through dedication and persistence?

The findings of one well-known study challenged the notion that we possess an innate, hidden calling waiting to be discovered. Instead, they concluded that any pursuit can become a calling when we engage with it and actively nurture our growth. Passions aren't stumbled upon; they're developed.[7] Another study in the realm of entrepreneurship found that the more effort people put into their ventures, the stronger their passion becomes.[8]

So, our passions aren't typically fully formed and waiting to be stumbled upon. A suitable analogy can be found in relationships. While the romantic idea of love at first sight is well-known, in reality, relationships often evolve gradually. We all know that this can be a non-linear process with its ups and downs, which makes it even more interesting and intriguing, doesn't it?

Reflection Point

Take some time to reflect and summarize your thoughts regarding your current situation with interests:
1. What is currently the main field of your professional interests? Which industry, its aspects, and niches?
2. Hypotheses: Which professional topics seem to spark interest but require further research and prototyping?

3. What dreams and ideas have come up that you'd like to explore safely?

If you don't have an answer to the first question, focus on 2 and 3, as they are sources of hypotheses. This will help organize your thoughts and see a more complete picture.

Key Points

- When you delve into the "What is my passion?" question, keep in mind that your first instinct might be to seek something entirely different, as far away as possible from your current job.
- Also, remember that ideas and light-bulb moments are not definitive answers; they are merely hypotheses. Even your dreams are just hypotheses.
- The answer might be very close but still not on your radar. Try stepping out of your usual work zone and see what's out there. Use 3x3x3 tool to explore different possibilities.
- Passion involves not only *what* you do, but also *how* you do it. Remember that what makes you happy in your career may evolve over time, rather than staying the same forever.

Chapter 3. What Do I Really Want and Where Am I Headed?

I met Feng at an alumni club where I was invited to run a workshop on finding meaning in work. After our initial chat, Feng connected with me on LinkedIn and suggested we have a Zoom coffee meeting.

When we met, he told me his story, which you are already a bit familiar with from the beginning of the book. Feng hailed from an immigrant family and carried the substantial weight of expectations. His parents wanted him to succeed. "My parents invested not just everything they had, but more than that, in my upbringing," he reflected. "They were my unwavering support system every step of the way." Feng's academic journey was marked by excellence, both in school and college. He started his first business at the age of 17, which was an online store selling funny socks and ties. Over time, he went on to found several startups, although not all of them achieved success.

A few years ago, he co-founded a fintech startup, which they later sold to a larger corporation. Feng was especially proud of buying a small, comfy house for his parents with the money he made.

When integration process had started, Feng had been offered a senior leadership role in the new company. However, as the integration process continued, he couldn't help but notice the once-vibrant startup culture slowly diminishing. With each passing month, his sense of discomfort grew more pronounced. He confided, "There are times when I wonder if something is wrong with me. Sarah, who was also a co-founder of our startup, seems to enjoy playing at a bigger scale and integrating into a new culture."

Nevertheless, he knows how to make things happen, and his results were great. Recently, his boss started a conversation about him leading a new innovative project within the company.

"I wake up and go to bed every day with the same question: Should I stay or should I go? How do I understand what is right for me, which direction is my direction?"

How Do You Figure Out What's Right for You?

To understand what's right for you, we need to first determine what kind of career success you consider *real success*, and what kind of achievements you believe are worth pursuing. In other words, we need to uncover your *personal vision of success*.

What constitutes success differs for each of us. Success is a highly individualized concept[1]. For some, it's leading a large corporation, while others might turn down promotions in favor of work-life balance. Some may establish a chain of stores, while others opt for a cozy café. Some may deliver speeches to crowds of thousands, while others find contentment in hosting Sunday dinners with friends.

Career fulfillment means shaping your path to fit your own vision of success. It's not about meeting standard expectations; it's about living up to your own and pursuing the goals that matter to you.

If you have a clear picture of what success is worth pursuing, it gives you the best orienting point possible. This point will help you understand what matters and make the choices that are right for you.

So, how do you figure it out?

Reflection Point

To better understand your concept of success, it's valuable to analyze your current role models—those individuals whose achievements inspire you and who embody your idea of a great career.

Step 1: Think about which style of ambition resonates more with you. Identify three to five examples of people who represent your idea of a great and meaningful career path. They can be from any field. Consider what it is about their stories that appeals to you the most.

Even if only well-known figures come to mind, that's okay. For example, J.K. Rowling might appear on different people's lists for different reasons. In one case, she's there because she "created an amazing new world and shared it with people," in another because she "pursued her dream despite all the challenges and hardships," and in a third because she "successfully monetized in a very unprofitable field." Notice? One role model, three meanings.

Step 2: Create a contrasting list. Identify two to three accomplished individuals whose success, while acknowledged as significant, doesn't personally resonate with you. It's essential to remember that these individuals can be exceptional in their own right, but their achievements don't serve as a source of inspiration for you.

Feng's roster of heroes from the first list included several names whose success he described as "creator of a product that positively impacted the industry" (first), "followed varying passions and created meaningful impact across multiple fields" (second), and "an innovator and creator of a series of breakthrough products that really changed the world" (third).

In the contrasting list, Feng detailed three accomplished businessmen. Regarding all of them, he remarked, "It's essentially a daily game of politics and chess, chasing power, characterized by extreme stress and little room for creativity."

Step 3: Take a moment to reflect on your lists and consider what they signify. How does the second list emphasize the message of the first list? Then summarize your thoughts on your current concept of success. Think about what kind of achievements would be meaningful for you personally, what kind of recognition is the right recognition, and what roles are the right roles for you in this picture.

Next time Feng was speaking from a hotel room in Singapore, where he was on a business trip. He said he always thinks better while traveling, so he had time to reflect on his answers: "What I see, and it resonates hugely, is that my concept of success is being a serial entrepreneur who creates groundbreaking innovations in various fields. My products are large-scale and have an impact on people's health, well-being, or prosperity. I lead strong teams, united by a powerful idea."

Then I asked him how he sees his current crossroads now.

"It really put things into perspective!" he said. "Now I can look at the current situation not from the point within it, but as if I have a reference point to check my path against."

That's exactly what was needed—finding that orienting point. It's like spotting the North Star brightly shining in the night sky, providing a clear sense direction to travelers. The North Star remains fixed in a constantly spinning world, a dependable point of reference when other landmarks are nowhere in sight.

Your North Star

Let's take a moment to break down and understand how the orienting point works.

It works as a guiding light: Once you discover your career North Star, you'll always have a clear heading. It serves as a guiding light that empowers you to navigate your career journey, making more authentic choices. For example, imagine you're presented with a new job opportunity. You can assess its alignment with your orienting point. Does it move you closer to your North Star, or does it pull you in the opposite direction?

It helps recalculate the route: Your North Star allows for route recalculation. Knowing your true aspirations enables you to find alternative paths even when things go awry. In Feng's words, "Now, even if I take a detour, I won't lose my path. I've always got the orientation point to steer myself right back on track."

It gives a sense of purpose and keeps us motivated: Knowing that what we do today leads us toward our vision of success is key for staying motivated, especially with long-term goals. It gives our actions meaning and pushes us forward. Think about tough times in running your own business or facing challenges in your corporate role. When you keep your goals in perspective, even the hard times won't get you down.

Our North Star changes over time. Often, we continue to pursue old goals without realizing they are no longer relevant or meaningful to us.

When I started my career, my North Star was becoming a corporate top executive. My role models were people who made big decisions and were valued for their intellect and responsibility. I played that game, but over time, these heroes faded, and they were replaced by independent professionals who help people and companies. My North Star changed, and I didn't realize it immediately; for a while, I continued climbing the career ladder out of habit.

After several years of practice and moving toward my new orienting point, another important shift happened. My North Star gained an important component: being an educator. My heroes became people who are not only experts but also authors, teachers, and active sharers of knowledge.

Understanding this dynamic can explain the logic behind your previous decisions, the loss of motivation at different stages of your journey, or the emerging feeling that you are heading in the wrong direction.

Reflection Point

Think about who would have been your heroes and antiheroes if you had answered this question five years ago, or at the start of your career, or at various turning points.

Reflect on when the last shift happened. When did your current role models appear? When did the concept of success they embody become relevant to you?

Reflecting on these questions, Feng came to understand that his old idea of success was all about scale. His heroes were the big players, and that's why he took the offer from the large company. But now he sees that scale alone isn't enough—he also needs freedom and impact.

"I realized I'm not playing my own game right now," he said. "Leaving or staying isn't a tough choice anymore; I know what's right for me."

Our perception of professional success is changing, and individuality is taking the forefront. There are no longer clearly defined trajectories, unequivocal success algorithms, and one-size-fits-all paths. And that's the key: craft your career in the configuration that aligns with your own vision of success.

So, let's stop measuring ourselves by other people's metrics. I want all of us to forge your own path, one that no one else will lay out for us. And even the maps won't be handed to us—we'll draw them as we go along. And whether we're moving quickly or slowly, that will also be entirely up to us. We're all the main characters in our own life stories.

Key Points

- What is right for me? What do I really want? What matters? The answer is your personal and subjective understanding of success applied to your life.
- It works as the North Star—an orienting point giving you a sense of direction and shaping your decisions.
- It acts as a guiding light, allowing you to recalculate your route when necessary and helps you make better choices.
- Recognizing that our present actions are leading us toward our personal vision of success is crucial. This perspective not

WHAT'S NEXT?

only fuels our motivation but also bolsters our resilience, helping us navigate through setbacks and obstacles.

Chapter 4. "So, What's Next?"

A while back, you found yourself rethinking your career and asking 'what's next?', faced with your big questions and mixed feelings. We've come quite a way together since then.

First, we focused on 'who am I?' to better understand your professional identity so that you could grasp the self-concept that fuels your work in different roles.

Next, we tackled 'what is my passion?' to free yourself from myths and unworkable stereotypes regarding passions and interests, enabling you to view the answer from a fresh perspective.

Then, we tried to clarify what truly matters to you and identified your North Star, which gives you a sense of direction and a point of orientation.

Without this self-awareness, choosing the next stage in your career could feel like shooting in the dark. But now, you can make a well-informed decision about what comes next, based on your understanding of yourself.

As we approach the question of what comes next, let's start by looking at the types of decisions people with different career paths make when rethinking their journey.

The Six Categories of 'What's Next' Decisions

There are six types of career changes I observe in my practice working with mid-career professionals. Some of these changes are within the same professional direction, while others involve changing it entirely.

1. **Leveling Up**: When people are ready to climb higher in what they're already doing. This could mean stepping up to a bigger role at work, primarily vertical, such as a promotion to a new role with more responsibilities. It can also involve moving to a larger or more prestigious company, where even the same role requires more skills and responsibilities.

2. **Changing a Niche Within the Same Direction**: Same field, new playground. People stay in their field but find new inspiration in another niche within it. Examples include moving from FMCG marketing to tech marketing or from investment finance to sustainable finance.

3. **Changing the Type of Career Within the Same Direction**: Accumulated professional experience is repackaged in a new format. For example, shifting from a corporate job to self-employment or entrepreneurship in the same field, or from full-time employment to part-time.

4. **Redesigning a Current Job**: When people tweak their current positions to better fit who they are now and what they need to be happier. In short, it's about sticking with it but making it yours—crafting/reinventing the same role.

5. **Changing Direction**: All previous changes were within the same direction, but this one involves changing your functional expertise and starting anew in a new field. This could mean a radical change, such as switching professions or industries. Examples include moving from finance to product management, from lawyer to coding, or from logistics to nutritionist.
6. **Taking a Pause from the Game**: Some people decide to hit pause on their careers to focus on parenting, take a sabbatical, pursue new education, or simply take an exploratory break to try something new. They might come back to the same career or change direction as a result.

The magnitude of change across these six categories may vary significantly, ranging from subtle tweaks to complete career overhauls. When I share these categories with others, there's one question that invariably comes up:

"Isn't it supposed to be about a big leap?"

There's a common belief that a major change is the only way to start a new and improved chapter in your professional journey.

Of course, taking the leap always makes for a compelling story. The most memorable tales often start with a bold move. *The sales director opened a hotel in Bali* – wow! *From a corporation to his own startup* – now, that's a jump! *He left everything to become an artist* – and the list goes on.

A prevailing myth suggests that only major changes can lead to something better. Yet, often the most impactful shifts are so subtle they might not even seem like changes at all. Why? Because the main task here, at turning point, not 'to change your career' but to find the *change you need*.

Remember Amir, the designer? He felt like he lost his creative touch. He decided to adjust the entry criteria for incoming projects, ensuring that at least half of them had room for creative expression. He also joined a community of creative designers—as he put it then, 'just for fun'. When we caught up a year later, he shared details about his new projects and how he had expanded his network with intriguing colleagues. "Man, it's like I've landed on a different planet with this job. I mean, I'm still slinging designs, but it feels like a whole other game".

Amir's story is a good example of **Redesigning a Current Job** —and it shows how even a small shift in the right place can ripple through the whole work. That's because the most significant change he needed was to activate his artistic potential, which had been suppressed before.

Would quitting his current career and move into something entirely different, such as becoming an architect, be beneficial for him? Maybe, maybe not. I think of Christina, who found herself at a turning point, burned out from her job in IT. She transitioned to hotel management, only to find herself in yet another cycle of burnout two years later, grappling with the same set of pressing questions. She thought that changing her job was the only change she needed. Unfortunately, that major transition didn't make a difference. Successful transitions aren't just about making big leaps. We're not seeking change just to change. We are looking for change that works for us.

Since we've already started illustrating categories with examples, let's go back to the beginning of the list. Here's an example for **Leveling Up**. Meet Alex, a project manager who had been leading his finance team for quite a while. He began to sense that he was hitting a professional plateau, and this marked the beginning of his "What's next?" moment. During this time, he realized he looked up to people in his field who were a few rungs higher up the ladder. He focused on landing a more strategic and influential role, taking inspiration from the Financial Controllers and CFOs in his domain. Alex decided to further his education in strategic finance and leadership, positioning himself as the top candidate for future senior-level opportunities. Also, let's take a look at Kate, a self-employed strategy consultant. For some time, she had felt bored and stagnant at her current level. In her career rethinking process, she decided to aim higher, targeting larger projects and significantly higher fees. To make this happen, she had to step up her game, so she refined her personal brand, invested in further education, and expanded her network to unlock exciting new opportunities and valuable connections.

WHAT'S NEXT?

Remember Lisa, a seasoned marketing specialist? Her story is a good example of **Changing a Niche Within the Same Direction** type of decision. She had built a successful career in marketing. During her 'what's next?' phase, she explored different niches and rediscovered the world of marketing, and while developing the idea of becoming an evangelist, she found a niche that resonated with her completely—green marketing. Now, she's using her marketing skills to promote sustainable energy solutions, raise awareness about environmental issues, and drive positive change.

For the next category, **Changing the Type of Career Within the Same Direction,** I serve as a pretty good case. I transitioned from a corporate role in talent management to working independently. It was a significant and occasionally daunting change, but it turned out to be exactly what worked for me. With years of experience to bring to the table, I started on solid ground instead of going from scratch.

In the next type of 'what's next' decision—**Changing Direction**—the magnitude of change is much bigger, because now we are talking about changing industry or profession. Examples here are people who started from scratch in something completely new, different from their previous careers: transitioning from technology to art, from mathematics to fashion, or from product management to becoming a chef. One of these people is Robert, who transitioned from auditing to landscape design, specializing in green walls. Landscape design was his hypothesis during his career rethinking process; he had no prior experience, but the topic seemed interesting to him, so he decided to test it by taking a course. Each step in this field generated even more interest, and after a year of balancing his day job and his new passion, he transitioned to the new field full-time. Four years later, he founded his own company.

And for final type of 'what's next' decision—**Pause from the game**—a fitting example is Feng, a serial entrepreneur well-known to you, who aspired to develop groundbreaking innovations with a significant impact. Seeking inspiration for his next big idea, Feng decided to spend a few months traveling across the world to connect with great minds and recharge with new ideas. Feng's plan was not just a vacation; it was a meticulously crafted sabbatical aimed at rejuvenating his mind. He plans to attend workshops, participate in think tanks, and join informal meet-ups with local innovators. In another example, Emily, a software engineer, chose to step away from her demanding job to focus on her newborn child. She wanted to be fully present during the first year of her child's life, believing that these moments were fleeting and irreplaceable.

We've talked about different kinds of 'what's next?' career choices. Now, let's dive into how to make these choices, because there's more to it than meets the eye.

The Decision Point - Why Is It So Hard...?

When I ask people in my lectures about the biggest risk at the turning point, most say it's making the wrong choice. It feels true, especially for those going for big changes.

But what I think, as a practitioner who observed thousands of career crossroads, the biggest risk is *getting stuck at the turning point*, overthinking.

Why?

There are three reasons.

First, when you spend too much time making decisions, it drains your energy because of cognitive load[2] and can lead to a state of mind known as mental fatigue[3], and "analysis paralysis." That's when you're so overwhelmed you'd do anything just to make a decision and be done with it. But here's the problem: the longer you think, the more scared you get of making the wrong choice. The more you doubt yourself, causing both mental and emotional stress.

Here's reason number two: overthinking feeds the FOMO (Fear of Missing Out) syndrome and makes you painfully aware of the opportunities you might be giving up. When you're stuck in decision-mode, you start noticing all the cool things others are doing. Someone's starting a new business, someone's climbing the career ladder, someone is switching jobs, and you might feel like you're just letting time slip away.

Finally, when you're stuck making a decision, it can undermine your self-esteem. Nothing's changing, self-doubt just keeps piling up, and sometimes you even start feeling guilty for taking so long to make up your mind. You might start thinking you're just not cut out to make the right choices. When you see everyone around you moving forward in life while you're stuck, it can make you feel inadequate.

But what about the risk of taking the wrong turn?

Well, it's actually quite minimal if you stick to one crucial rule: when you're aiming for major changes, start by exploring and prototyping.

Exploring and Prototyping

Carla, a lawyer, dreamed of resigning one day to write a bestseller. Quitting a job is a significant decision, but if writing truly captivated her heart, it was worth considering. Before immersing herself in the world of writing, I suggested she spend a two-week vacation living the life of a full-time writer. In just one week, she realized that solely writing wasn't stimulating enough; life should offer more variety. Her next insight was that she could incorporate writing into almost any schedule, even if it's just for 30 minutes a day. This amounts to 3.5 hours a week dedicated to crafting her book. Spending two weeks "as if it were already her profession" served as a beneficial test drive.

Max, an architect, aspired to be a film director. He started exploring this path by attending a hands-on seminar for aspiring directors. Wanting a deeper understanding of what the job entails, he enrolled in a 14-week intensive film directing course in Hollywood. Several months later, reflecting on everything he had learned about the profession while creating his prototypes, Max decided to invest in a full-time film education at a prestigious school, fully committing to his new direction.

Nina, a project manager intrigued by entrepreneurship and considering it as a possible 'what's next?' decision, chose to explore this hypothesis by networking with startup founders and participating in a weekend startup bootcamp. The chaotic startup scene made her realize she preferred the stability of her corporate job. However, she was excited to bring her newfound entrepreneurial knowledge back to her role, making it more fulfilling.

Now, let's talk about Lars, who worked as a supply chain manager. He decided to dip his toes into entrepreneurship by starting a small e-commerce business on the side, just to test the waters. As his little side project started gaining momentum, Lars felt a new energy and motivation that had been missing in his corporate role. Fast forward six months, and Lars made a bold decision—he resigned from his corporate position to fully commit to his e-commerce business. He was ready to take the leap.

What Are We Really Tasting There?

Through prototyping, you assess not only your interest in the topic but, more importantly, you explore *the possible selves* we discussed in the "Who am I?" chapter. Carla tested her writer self, Max tested his film director self, and Nina and Lars tested their entrepreneurial selves.

To test your entrepreneurial self, you may consider starting a small, independent project where you're in control, you set the tasks and deadlines, creating your own structure. The responsibility is all yours. This project could be anything: a blog, an online store, a podcast series, event organizing, consultancy, or even writing a book — the decision is yours.

Even if the idea of working for yourself seems incredibly appealing, it's crucial to first test yourself in this format. Don't fall into the common misconception that becoming your own boss automatically leads to fulfillment and happiness.

A story from my mailbox: "I've been running my own business for the past few years, but I closed it this year. When I started, and even while I was managing it, I believed that working for myself meant making all my own decisions, not having to depend on bosses, having no limits to my earnings and growth, enjoying a flexible schedule, and working on my own time. However, the reality also included a constant rush without breaks during weekends or evenings, overwhelming routine tasks, and an inability to focus on long-term strategic matters. I faced income uncertainty, competitive, economic, and political risks, and the necessity to do things I don't enjoy and am less skilled at, which overshadowed my strengths. Besides, I felt isolated, missing out on communication and the chance to learn from others.'"

Another one expressed, "My main fear was being stuck in corporate slavery, but I ended up becoming a slave to my own business without even noticing." So, yes, it does happen.

On Career Prototyping

Major career changes come with many uncertainties. "What if I don't like this?" "What if my project fails and I've already quit my job?" "What if this isn't for me and it's too late to change?" Career prototyping is a way to reduce these risks and pay a very small price for an experiment.

The goals of the prototype are verification, experimentation, and new information without commitments. There's no such thing as failure here because you'll achieve these goals regardless.

A good prototype has four characteristics:
1. It evokes positive emotions, not paralyzing fear.
2. It explorative and isn't just about overthinking old data.
3. It's relatively small and inexpensive: requires little time, money, and energy (fail cheap, fail fast).
4. It's free of commitment.

"No, I don't need to test anything; I'm sure this is for me" is a common mistake and a false clarity. Remember the cautionary tale of Alexander with the restaurant of his dreams. *Remember: going for idea you're 100% sure about without prototyping inevitably creates a prototype, but a very expensive one.*

How to Make Sense of Your Experiments

Here's a set of questions that can guide you through reflecting on your experience:

- Did your interest in the idea or topic grow?
- What insights did you gain about yourself and how you acted in this trial run?
- Which of your initial expectations were met, and what aspects turned out to be completely different from what you anticipated?
- Did any new role models or projects catch your attention?

Remember, prototyping is all about learning, so every outcome, whether expected or not, is valuable. People often think that if their initial hypothesis doesn't hold up, the experiment was a failure. But that's not true. Even when things don't go as planned, you end up learning something new about yourself, which is always a positive result.

Here are some more examples of outcomes from prototyping.

"When I shadowed my mentor for a day, I realized that a high-influence role in the company requires a different version of me, and I didn't like it."

"I attended the first workshop on this topic and within five minutes, I felt the most like myself and in my tribe."

"Even a small side project showed me how important it is for me to be part of a team; I will not enjoy the role of a lone wolf roaming the market plains."

"During the COVID pandemic, I tried on the hat of a self-employed professional, which was almost a perfect fit due to the home office format, since I spent my days alone except for conference calls. While everyone else was missing human interaction, I enjoyed."

"After the first outing as a guide, it became clear that I had romanticized the role too much—I'm not a nanny, I'm not a pusher, I'm not a porter after all."

"Even this trial blog showed I can't motivate myself; I need some external control."

"After a volunteer project on strategy development, I understood which part of the strategy is appealing and which isn't for me. Also I discovered two role models who's examples inspires me now."

So, what's next? Now let's go back to the list of 'what's next?' decisions and decide which one of them will be relevant for your next stage.

Key Points

- There are six types of "What's next?" decisions:
  Leveling Up
  Changing a Niche Within the Same Direction
  Changing the Type of Career Within the Same Direction
  Redesigning a Current Job
  Changing Direction
  Taking a Pause from the Game

- It's not always about making a big leap. The main task at the turning point is not necessarily 'to change your career,' but to find the change you need.
- The bigger the decision and the more unknowns it contains, the more important it is to test the idea first.
- By prototyping, you evaluate not only your interest in the topic but, more importantly, you try on possible future selves.
- Prototyping is a learning process, meaning any result—positive or negative—is valuable.

Chapter 5: Big 'Ifs'

Let's dive into the three most common doubts I see when people are figuring out their next steps:
1. "What if I am making a mistake?"
2. "What if I am not good enough for that?"
3. "What if it's too late to change something?"

Big Doubt #1: "What if I Am Making a Mistake?"

Picture this: My last day as a corporate talent manager. There I was, at my desk, feeling like a clock was ticking down on me. It felt like prepping for a skydive with a parachute I wasn't quite sure about. As I looked across the office and saw everyone immersed in their work, that feeling just grew stronger. Then came the final chat with my boss, Raymond – a mix of a pep talk and farewell advice – which somehow made me even more jittery about the leap I was about to take.

My flight to Paris was just two days away! The dream, the big move, all waiting for me. My ticket to a new life was literally in my pocket, and a charming apartment near the Place de la Madeleine was all set up. You'd think I'd be over the moon. But to my surprise, I wasn't!

The day after the farewell, for some reason, I found myself back at the business center, at the cafe where I always bought coffee before work. I didn't travel across half the city; I lived nearby. I repeated my daily morning ritual: I bought my usual latte. I drank it while watching the beautiful, confident people rushing to their stable and, of course, wonderful jobs. Then I threw away the empty cup and wandered home, where only the remaining preparations for my Paris suitcases calmed and distracted me.

I recall these feelings every time one of my clients shares their fears and doubts on the threshold of a new career stage. They often consider these doubts and fears as signs of making a mistake. But here's the thing: the presence of doubts and fears is just a sign of being human. It is not a marker of mistakes.

Researchers have long been studying the complex nature of decision-making, and all the emotions associated with it[1]. The bigger the decision, the larger the emotional effect. I always advise those I work with, especially those at pivotal moments in their careers, to be prepared for what I call 'fear tides'—sudden surges of doubt and anxiety on the path to change. It's important to face these emotions head-on, acknowledging them as a normal part of the process. Acceptance and creating space for these feelings are crucial.

Imagine this: just yesterday, you were full of plans and ideas, but then, in the middle of the night, you're suddenly awake, haunted by doubts like, 'What if it was all just an illusion?' It's common to feel confident in your new role one day, only to grapple with fears of making a mistake the next morning. Recognizing and accepting these emotional ups and downs as a natural part of your career journey is key to ensuring they don't knock you off course.

Total Certainty is Unattainable

Many people mistakenly believe that a new stage in their career should start with zero doubt and complete certainty. We crave clarity and certainty, especially at career turning points, because the stakes feel high. The further we progress in our careers, the more we tend to weigh the costs of each decision heavily.

However, the reality is that total certainty is unattainable. Even prototyping does not fully guarantee that everything will work out. Absolute certainty is impossible because life is unpredictable. New technologies emerge, the political and economic context changes, the job market shifts, new professions arise, and old ones disappear. As we grow in our careers, our own changes add to this uncertainty. Our skills, interests, and what we value can change, affecting what we want from our careers. Big life events like having a family, moving, or rethinking our life goals also shape our career choices and their results.

So, don't be hard on yourself for not being 100% certain.

On Status Quo Bias

Not only that, but staying in one place is no necessarily the safer option. Opting to keep everything as is can be just as risky as deciding to make a change. There's even a term for this phenomenon: "status quo bias."[2] This essentially means we have a tendency to cling to our current job or career track, even when change might lead to better outcomes. This bias can hold us back from exploring new opportunities or taking next steps.

Once I had a client who was an engineer at a big retail company. A tech startup offered him a great job. He spent a long and agonizing time weighing all the options, all the pros and cons, and ultimately he rejected the offer, thinking it was safer to stay where he was. Later, when the economy got tough, he lost his job anyway.

The false security associated with leaving everything as it is doesn't work. The risk will be the same, as strange as it may sound. We can't be certain either way. If changes are overdue, it's worth moving forward.

What Is Your Tolerance to Uncertainty?

Uncertainty affects everyone differently—some are all right with it, while others feel almost paralyzed by it. This difference stems from genetic, psychological, sociocultural, and environmental factors[3]. Some people really struggle with the idea that life is full of unknowns, so if you're someone who finds uncertainty hard to handle, many situations can feel overwhelming.

Researchers have created a method to measure how much uncertainty bothers and even impairs you, known as the 'Intolerance of Uncertainty Scale.'[4] It asks you to agree or disagree with statements such as: 'It's unfair not to have guarantees in life,' 'I can't relax my mind if I don't know what will happen tomorrow,' 'It frustrates me not to have all the information I need,' 'Uncertainty paralyzes me when it's time to act,' and 'When I am uncertain, I can't function very well'.

If you take this quiz and find out your intolerance of uncertainty is high, does that mean you can't deal with change? Not at all. It just means you might need to take smaller, safer steps when making changes, especially if you're someone who feels more at ease knowing what's ahead.

One of my clients, Carina, a super achiever who struggles with uncertainty, is now successfully expanding her local business to the international scene. The transition of her business looked like a huge, frightening leap into the unknown in an uncontrollable environment. She's doing it step by step, feeling okay with each move, and now she is at a level that just thinking about used to make her dizzy and her pulse jumped.

We don't need full certainty, and moreover, it is impossible. What we need is *enough certainty* and motivation to take the first steps into our next stage. 'Enough' will be different for each of us. But there are two signals of enough certainty: your idea of what's next makes sense to you, and you want to take those first steps.

My favorite story about doubts and fears is related to Irina, a successful cheesemaker. Before her cheese career, she worked successfully in a bank for 20 years, and her new chapter began with a small step: she ordered a home cheesemaking kit. The second step was a career prototype—a trip to study at a private Italian creamery. For the next couple of years, she continued to make cheese in parallel with her main job. Eventually, her passion led her to open her own creamery and store. There, she encountered a moment that she shared with me:

> "Hey Lena, just yesterday, a guy from nearby, also interested in cheesemaking, dropped by my shop. He bombarded me with doubts: 'Wasn't it terrifying to quit your stable job?' 'What if the electricity goes out, what happens to the cheese?' 'What if the landlords kick you out?' 'What if your cheesemakers leave?'
> What if... What if... I told him that I'm also afraid. But he's scared sitting in an office, and I'm scared in my own creamery."

You Don't Need to Know the Entire Route in Advance

Many achievers feel uneasy with just the first few steps; they crave a longer, clearer, fixed, step-by-step plan. It gives them a sense of control. Starting a new career stage without a rigid comprehensive plan seems like inviting disaster.

I've seen a lot of worry about not having a detailed, long-term career plan. But honestly, having such a plan might be more concerning. It's like having a move-by-move chess strategy planned out in advance – no matter how thorough it is, it quickly becomes useless after the game begins.

Traditional planning works well in stable, predictable situations. That's why I suggest using it for things like health habits, learning languages, or sports training. But for careers, we need a different approach.

The chess metaphor seems suitable for the career context—we act step by step, considering the changing situation after each move and calculating the associated opportunities and risks. We cannot get lost because—remember?—we have a reference point, our North Star.

This approach is based on the concept of equifinality, which means there are many ways to reach the same goal. There isn't just one right path to success. One person might climb the corporate ladder at their company to reach a top position, while another might move between industries or take breaks for personal growth and still end up at the same level of success. This shows that everyone's career path is unique and we should stay open to different opportunities that can lead us where we want to go.

If there's not just one right way to reach a goal, you don't need to stress over creating a perfect, detailed plan from the start. Having such a plan can actually be risky, as it might lead to sticking with it too rigidly, a problem known as 'plan continuation bias'.

Don't Fall in Love with Plans

Laurence Gonzales, a survival expert and author of *Deep Survival: Who Lives, Who Dies, and Why*, talks about "plan continuation bias." In tough situations, this means people might keep going down a risky path instead of stopping to think and change their approach. Gonzales says this happens partly because people really believe in their first plan and don't like the uncertainty of changing the route. For example, mountain climbers might be so focused on reaching the top that they ignore bad weather or how tired they are. This "summit fever" can lead to bad choices and even deadly situations.

It's easy to get locked into a set plan, and even when faced with cues that suggest changing course, we fail to do so. It's okay if your plan changes. As long as you know your main goal, your North Star, you can always recalculate and find a new way to get there.

When Big Plans Fail, Micro-Planning Rules

I would like to share one unusual strategy that works well in the process of change. It might seem odd considering everything said earlier about plans, but it helps bring back a sense of control during transitions. This strategy is micro-planning. By micro-planning, I mean the meticulous planning of a day, a week, or a month, with mandatory marking off of everything completed. The greater the anxiety and uncertainty, the more detailed the items on your to-do list should be. I've had days when I checked off 'organize my work desk' or 'go through the slides for tomorrow's presentation again'.

I've noticed this strategy works exceptionally well for my clients. It makes sense because they are used to maintaining control and consistently hitting their goals. Losing that sense of control, which is a key part of change, can feel really disempowering. As our brain can't tell the difference between big and small senses of control, micro planning and celebrating small wins takes power back.

Big Doubt #2. "What If It's Too Late to Change Something?"

I've met people in their 50s who felt like they were just beginning, and others in their 30s who said it's all downhill from here. Late or not late really depends on how you see things.

Sadly, a popular concept of professional success prescribes the idea that the earlier you attain the summit, the better. Are you caught in the trap of thinking it's already too late? Let me ask you something simple.

Imagine you're 35. Have you ever truly grasped the fact that you've got a solid 30 years of career ahead of you? That's double what you've already done. Even if you start all over, you could have a new one, or even more than one, successful career during that time. Have you ever thought about it from this point of view?

And let's not forget the global trend: careers are extending far beyond what we once believed possible. We're steadily moving towards an era of working well into our seventies. So, at the age of 35, don't limit your forecast to a mere three decades; it's more plausible that you've got several additional years to conquer. This should be exciting! Investing in education or new skills pays off in the long run.

Think about your very first day at work. Look at all you've achieved since then. There was probably a lot that felt impossible back then. Now, think of today as the first day of the second half of your career. But now, you're smarter, cooler, and more experienced than before. Who would I bet on? I'd bet on you, right now, without a second thought.

Is this convincing enough? I have more to tell.

Debunking the Early Success Myth

Rich Karlgaard, in his book *Late Bloomers: The Power of Patience in a World Obsessed with Early Achievement*, tells us that research on the brain and ageing shows we keep our creative skills and original thinking almost until the end of life. He challenges the cultural obsession with early achievement and the idea that if you haven't achieved significant success early in life, you're less likely to do so at all. He says many people develop their talents and find their direction later in life, but society's focus on early success often misses these individuals' potential.

The idea that we reach an intellectual peak early, followed by a gradual decline in abilities, is fundamentally wrong. In fact, most of us experience a multitude of cognitive peaks throughout our lives.

As for entrepreneurs, contrary to the popular belief that young people are most likely to create successful new firms, data on entrepreneurs reveal that the average age of business founders whose companies achieve success is around 40 years old. This insight comes from 'Age and High-Growth Entrepreneurship' research conducted by MIT professor Pierre Azoulay.[5] Developmental psychologist Erik Erikson's work supports the idea that the peak of entrepreneurial activity often occurs in one's early forties.[6] He wrote that the period from forty to sixty-four represents a unique time when creativity and experience combine with the universal human desire to make the world a better place.

Dean Keith Simonton, in his study 'Age and Outstanding Achievement: What Do We Know After a Century of Research?'[7] talks about 'career age', which is how long you've been in your field. He suggests that achievements have more to do with the duration of your career rather than your age. The best productivity often comes between 15 and 30 years into your career.

Here's more great news: as we get further along in our careers, we develop a new strength known as *crystallized intelligence*[8]. This is our brain's collection of all the knowledge and skills we've gained over time – like a library of facts, how-to knowledge, and wisdom from our work. As we get older, this library keeps growing. Think of it like a chef who doesn't need recipes anymore and can whip up amazing dishes just by knowing their ingredients and relying on their past cooking experience. This wealth of knowledge and experience is super useful, especially when solving complex problems or making big decisions.

Consider, for instance, Dana. At 56, she's a standout in strategic consulting. With many years of experience in different industries, she has a vast knowledge of market trends, how businesses work, and how organizations function. This deep understanding helps her solve complex business problems and provide valuable advice that only someone with her level of expertise can offer. As a result, she has become a sought-after expert, helping companies tackle difficult challenges and make wise decisions.

Here's another example: Miguel, a retired high school geography teacher, has always had a passion for the environment. He used to spend his weekends exploring nearby trails and documenting the local plants and wildlife. At the age of 57, driven by his wish to spread his love and appreciation for nature to others, Miguel started an eco-tourism project. Leveraging his teaching experience, Miguel designed tours that were not just informative but also engaging and educational.

Unusual Tool to Overcome the 'Too Late' Mindset

Here's a tool that has worked for me and many others who think it's already too late to change anything. This tool is a picture of the regrets you might have in the future. For me, this image naturally came as a recurring nightmare about my old age. A hospital, air saturated with the smell of medicines, a white ceiling. Tubes all around, IV drips, barely enough strength to shuffle to the bathroom. I am profoundly and quietly miserable. Not because of old age, but because I understand that life is ending. But did it ever begin? I was terrified by this image of an elderly and frail me, who, at the end of life, suddenly realizes that all the previous years were like a rough draft because I never dared to do what I wanted. I never gave myself a chance. I never tried to live on my own terms. The scariest part of this picture was that it was too late to change anything.

This scary vision motivated me more than anything else when I was about to make my big changes. It was a stronger push than the idea of what I might gain. This isn't surprising. The fear of regretting an unlived life can be more powerful than the fear of change, even at forty. The power of regret is a great force and a valuable source of insight[9].

The doubt about whether it's too late or not goes beyond just your career; it's about your entire life. This doubt can have enormous defining power, and its impact can be devastating. Addressing this doubt is not limited to the content of this chapter, but the key is to recognize that it exists. Once you do, you can change the situation. In the end, it's all about you and only you deciding when it's too late, not anyone else.

Big Doubt #3: "What If I Am Not Good Enough?"

Feeling like you're not good enough is pretty common when you're moving from one stage of your career to another. It's a time when vulnerability really spikes, and that's just the way it goes.

In any big change, there will be moments when you doubt yourself and your abilities. This is just part of the journey when you're moving from one stage of your career to the next. Of course, one would like to go through the entire journey with unwavering self-confidence, always being strong, never doubting one's abilities, and feeling proud of oneself for being brave and embarking on something new. But reality is, along the transition, there will inevitably be times when we lack full confidence in ourselves and our ability to achieve our goals.

Think of it like a crab shedding its shell. Crabs reach a point when they outgrow their old shell and have to leave it behind to grow a new, bigger one. Without their shell, crabs are soft and vulnerable. They're the same crab, but without the hard protection they're used to. What a great metaphor for major career changes!

Career change it's always about spending time somewhere between your old self and the new self, in between, in the middle of nowhere.[10] Scholars have a special term for that—liminality.[11]

In simple terms, liminality means being in a transitional phase, where you're not quite what you used to be and not yet what you will become. Uncertainty, both external and internal, during the liminal period skyrockets, creating a sense of complete disorientation.

The Pressure to Be Perfect

You'd think the uncertainty of change alone would make us doubt ourselves. But there's more to it – we're living in a time where there's an extreme pressure to be perfect, in everything. This era of high expectations and perfectionism makes us feel like we're never good enough, even if our lives are stable and we're not going through big changes.

Will Storr, a researcher and journalist, explains it simply: people feel something's wrong with them when they don't match up to an ideal version of themselves. Everywhere we look – on TV, YouTube, in magazines – we see images of confident, good-looking, independent, upbeat, hard-working, and socially responsible people. This makes us think we need to reach this high level. The message is clear: if you're not like this, you're not doing well enough. You have to be the best version of yourself to succeed. Storr and other researchers think this pressure to be perfect is causing more and more people to feel depressed.[12]

In our careers, we might always feel like we're not doing enough because of this pressure to be perfect all the time. During the transition period, outside the familiar shell of the old role, the feeling of one's own imperfection intensifies even further. It's as if a weight has been placed on a crab without its shell. This explains the intensification of the feeling of vulnerability during the transition period. But that's not all; some of you might encounter another factor.

Career Trauma

During times of career transition, old job-related traumas can come back stronger.

Here's a story told by a marketing specialist: "I once got a PR job at a retail store, covering for someone on maternity leave. But on my first day, she had to go to the hospital, and suddenly, I was thrown into the deep end. They said it was my chance to prove myself. I had no idea how tough it would be. I had to manage all the communications for a store opening, tirelessly working through day and night, even on weekends. Daily, I faced the shadow of my predecessor's success, constantly being reminded of how she excelled at everything I struggled with. I felt utterly useless and profoundly lost. Then came the day I made a significant error. Confessing to my boss, I hoped for understanding but was met with the stinging words that the woman I replaced, the true professional, would rectify my blunder. I wasn't fired, yet the humiliation was too much to bear, and I resigned. Months passed before I could muster the courage to consider job hunting again. Even now, just passing by those stores floods me with those haunting feelings of inadequacy and professional failure."

Psychologically, trauma is a response to a deeply upsetting event that affects your mental and emotional health. Career trauma does the same, damaging your professional confidence and self-esteem. Professionals carry these painful memories and hidden hurts, invisible to others but deeply wounding. Career trauma is more than just a bad experience. It alters your sense of self, imposes limits, and fills you with doubts and fears. It often resurfaces at the most inopportune moments, such as during a transition period when you most need to be at your strongest.

If you understand that you're carrying painful professional memories, remember, you're not alone in this and consider working through them with a psychologist.

As you can see, we all enter a career transition with different experiences—some with traumas, but most without. However, we all experience self-doubt during this time. This feeling is unpleasant, and we need to learn how to live through it without holding ourselves back. I have a method that has helped many of my clients and has repeatedly helped me as well.

Making Peace with Self-Doubt During Transitions

A goal, especially an important one, will always come at a price paid in the currency of doubt.

Take entrepreneurs, for instance. Starting a business involves being prepared to confront uncertainties, make errors, and occasionally feel a bit foolish. For writers, it's about signing up for the challenges along with the inspiration: the writer's block, the frustration with your text, the fear that it may not resonate. Sarting something new, we often focus only on the good things we expect from achieving our goals, but we don't prepare for that amount of self-doubts. That's completely normal. What we really need is to accept this as part of the process to keep stress at bay.

Here's a straight-up strategy: make a pact with yourself. Feel free to use this as a template and craft your own personalized version: *"I, [your name], am embarking on a path of change, and I wholeheartedly embrace the uncertainties and vulnerability that accompany it. I understand that these doubts and uncertainties aren't obstacles but an integral part of the journey of change. I am dedicated to facing these doubts with understanding and acceptance, acknowledging that they are a normal part of the process."*

As one of my clients told me, "I can't describe the relief I felt. So much time and energy were freed up! I realized that my doubts were just piling on more doubts. I used to think I needed to be 100% confident all the time and that any doubt meant something was really wrong. But now, I just let those doubts be, and it's become so much easier to move forward."

So, make the pact and make it official: date and sign it. Remind yourself of it whenever you start thinking that you're not good enough. You are enough; so just keep moving forward and stay on track.

Key Points

"What if I am making a mistake?"
- Uncertainty and 'fear tides' are normal in career transitions.
- Complete certainty is unrealistic. Don't expect it from yourself!
- Microplanning is a great tool to restore your sense of control amidst uncertainty.

"What if it's too late to change something?"
- Be aware of how the myth of early success and other stereotypes affect you and create the sense of 'too late.'
- Do your calculations and look at time from this perspective.
- The fear of future regret can be a powerful motivator for embracing change, even when it feels like it's too late.

"What if I am not good enough for that?"
- Experiencing self-doubt during career transitions is normal and can be likened to a crab shedding its old shell for a new one ('liminality' phase)'.
- High expectations and perfectionism adds to the pressure of career transitions.
- Making a pact to embrace self-doubts and normalize them as part of the transition can be a helpful strategy.

Part 2. Mastering Career Transitions

From Big Questions to Big Picture

Up until now, we've been focused on your current "what's next?" moment—getting to know yourself better, figuring out your next steps, and dealing with doubts.

But as we head into the second part of the book, we're going to shift perspectives and look at the bigger picture of a career path, and what makes us feel satisfied or not.

We're doing this because our goal isn't just to handle the current 'what's next?' moment but also to learn how to navigate these moments throughout your career and build more sustainable success overall.

Chapter 6. Learn to Navigate Transitions and Make the Most of Them

Multi-Staged Career as the Norm

Traditional careers used to have three stages: education, work, and retirement. Now, it's more of a multi-stage journey with transitions being the new norm, as Lynda Gratton and Andrew Scott write in their book "The 100-Year Life."

The career rethinking process you're currently navigating is far from your last. In the context of today's nonlinear, multi-stage career paths, these moments are inevitable. Some happen because you initiate them, and others are triggered by external events.

When your career shift comes from within, it's often because you're evolving and seeking a path that aligns with your current self. You might be craving a better work-life balance, aiming for new goals, or addressing feelings of burnout or dissatisfaction in your current role.

On the flip side, career crossroads often come from things outside your control. These can include new technologies changing your industry, big economic changes affecting your job market, major personal events like family needs or moving to a new place, or changes in what the job market needs. Both your personal goals and external events play a big role in shaping your career path.

Let's look at the stories of two people whose successful careers consisted of several stages, each beginning with a 'what's next?' moment followed by a transition to the next stage. You will see that even within a career in the same professional field, there can be many crossroads.

Maya's journey

Stage One: In the Corporate World

Maya began her journey in the finance sector working as a junior analyst at a bank. She dove into market analysis and her dedication and attention to detail quickly made her stand out as reliable and full of smart ideas. As Maya once said, "Back then, I was keen on progressing to higher-level roles." And she did just that. She worked her way up and became a well-respected senior financial advisor.

Stage Two: To sustainable investment

Ten years into her finance career, Maya started feeling like she needed a change. She was still into the finance game, but she wanted her work to mean something more, especially in something she really cared about. She made up her mind to put her finance smarts to good use in a new area: sustainable finance. She joined a firm specializing in sustainable investments, where she helped create financial products.

Stage Three: The entrepreneurial leap

The experience in sustainable finance ignited an entrepreneurial spark within Maya. She shared, "That experience really opened my eyes. It was challenging, exciting, and so fulfilling to take my passion and turn it into something that could really make a difference." She established her own consultancy, focused on providing sustainable financial solutions to businesses and nonprofits. At first, she teamed up with a partner, but things didn't work out between them. After going solo for a year, Maya decided it was time to grow. She brought on board three employees.

Stage Four: The parenting pause

While Maya was doing well professionally, she hit a huge personal milestone – becoming a mom to twins. She tried to balance work and motherhood, but found it too challenging. "I wasn't ready for this at all. It felt like I was losing grip on everything, and I had to make some really tough choices about what mattered most. It was the hardest time in my career..." Eventually, she handed over the affairs to the team and stayed on only in name.

Stage Five: The strategic return

With her kids growing up, Maya felt it was the right time to jump back into her professional life. Her break from work to focus on parenthood had left her rejuvenated and ready to tackle new challenges. She re-emerged with an offer from a leading fashion brand known for its sustainable practices. They offered her the role of Chief Financial Officer, and Maya found the opportunity too intriguing to pass up.

Maya's journey is ongoing and there is more to expect in the future.

Arthur's journey

Stage One: Self-employment

Arthur's career began not in an office, but from his home. With a mobility impairment, he found it tough to land a regular job as companies often overlooked his potential, focusing on his disability rather than his capabilities. "Self-employment had become practically the only available alternative," he said. He started as a freelance video editor and taught himself coding using online resources. During this period, his love for tech just kept growing. That passion led him to take things a step further and go for a degree in computer science.

Stage Two: Joining the tribe

With a mix of hands-on experience and academic knowledge under his belt, Arthur started making a name for himself as a talented developer. A tech company, attracted by his freelance work and problem-solving skills, hired him. At this company, Arthur wasn't just another employee; he was a vital part of the team, valued for his contributions and ideas. He once shared, "I felt like I found my tribe, and it was an amazing feeling."

Stage Three: Starting his own business

Years down the line, Arthur, now armed with plenty of experience and a strong network of colleagues, spotted a gap in the market for an app that would make technology more accessible for people with disabilities. Drawing from his own experiences, he designed an app that used adaptive technologies to help users navigate their devices more easily. With this innovation, Arthur started his own company with three partners.

Stage Four: The academic ascent

Four years into running his company, Arthur decided to delve even deeper into the world of technology and research. He coordinated his exit with his partners, remained as a board member, and took on the challenge of becoming a PhD student, focusing his studies on human-computer interaction. What really drove him was his passion for finding ways to make technology even more accessible for people with disabilities. "I was committed to pushing the boundaries and breaking down more barriers in this field."

This is clearly not the end of either Maya's or Arthur's story. Their careers, with varied stages and significant turning points, show us something important about how careers develop. Looking back, their paths might seem smooth and well-planned, but they both admit that every major change weren't easy decisions.

Maya: "Every time I thought about making a change, my mom and some friends would tell me it wasn't a good idea, and honestly, there were moments I felt like I was messing up big time. It was hard to see where I was going, and I often felt lost and unsure. But now, when I look back, my career looks like a jigsaw puzzle where every piece – whether it's about change, growth, or even those confusing times – fits perfectly, making sense in a way I never expected."

Arthur: "My career's been like a winding road, taking me through learning new things about myself, getting educated, working with others, and finally creating something that's really mine. I've learned that a career is something you can keep tweaking and improving, just like when you're coding – always adjusting and changing with new situations."

Making the Most of 'What's Next?' Moments

As Howard Stevenson from Harvard Business School put it, 'Very few people see inflection points as the opportunities they often are: catalysts to changing their lives; moments when a person can modify the trajectory and redirect it in a more desirable direction.'[1]

'What's next' moments are strategic points in our journey. We need them. They're our chance to change things up for the better, to evaluate our current career path in light of our long-term vision, and to align it with our true aspirations. Without these moments, we risk losing direction and wasting time and effort.

Imagine a hiker on a new route who never stops to check their direction. They'll likely end up lost, off on some random trail. In a career context, this is like taking on roles or projects that don't align with one's vision of success, leading to a career that feels unfulfilling or disjointed. 'What's next?' moments aren't just a break in motion; they're crucial times to make a mental step back and gain perspective. As Brad Stalberg notes in 'Master of Change,' it is about "being in conversation with change instead of it happening to you".[2]

Set the Next Review

Don't just sit back and wait for the next career fork to pop up—proactively set aside regular times to reflect on your career. I suggest doing it at least once a year. This way, you regularly check in on your career path and make adjustments as needed.

Adam Grant in his book *Think Again*[3] writes about the same approach as a 'career checkup': "My advice to students is to take a cue from health-care professions. Just as they make appointments with the doctor and the dentist even when nothing is wrong, they should schedule checkups on their careers. I encourage them to put a reminder in their calendars to ask some key questions twice a year. When did you form the aspirations you're currently pursuing, and how have you changed since then? Have you reached a learning plateau in your role or your workplace, and is it time to consider a pivot?"

At scheduled review points, you'll train yourself to view your career from a big-picture perspective. It helps you make the smartest choices, spot the best opportunities, and notice what truly matters.

Here's the agenda I suggest for scheduled big-picture reviews:

- Reflect on what you have learned about yourself since the last time you made a 'what's next?' decision.
- Assess where you are now in relation to your North Star.
- Decide if you want to change something or keep things as they are.
- Make a plan to prototype and experiment with new interests and ideas.

The main goal of these review points is to touch base with your current understanding of yourself and your definition of success. Since your last "what's next" decision, you've likely evolved. This self-assessment helps ensure your choices are in sync with who you are now, making them right for you.

If we only conduct these big-picture reviews when something happens—when we're already unhappy or at a dead end—we end up making career decisions under very stressful conditions and often with limited time frames. This, at least in part, explains why career turning points and transitions can be so scary and people are just white-knackeling this ride.

Think of this as a skill you can master, and it'll help you out again and again. The next time you hit a crossroad with big questions, it won't feel like a strange, unsettling moment.

Instead, you'll navigate it like a pro, because you'll be on familiar ground.

The Right-Sized Change

One of the most important parts of making the most out of career 'what's next?' moments is figuring out the right-sized change. Not just any change, but the right-sized one. This is the adjustment that will make your career truly work for you and enhance your overall satisfaction.

And this is where the 'all or nothing' bias trips us up.

The 'all or nothing' bias in decision-making is the belief that only extreme changes can lead to better satisfaction. It's like thinking, "I need to change everything because now it doesn't work." This mindset misses the power of smaller, more gradual adjustments. Sure, a major crisis might seem to demand major changes, but that's not always the case.

Let's take a corporate lawyer who is not happy in his job. Thinking that a big change is the only solution, he leaves his career to start a boutique bookstore, even though he knows little about retail. He puts a lot of time and money into this new business but soon realizes that it has its own challenges, which don't really match what he wants. The big change he made, hoping for happiness, doesn't give him the fulfillment he was looking for.

The right-sized change might be a minor tweak or a major shift, depending on what will best serve your career aspirations and needs. It's all about understanding your own situation and deciding what will bring you more fulfillment and engagement in your work. It's not as obvious as you might think.

Let me share a non-career example with you. A friend of mine told me that she had tried various diets and exercise routines to improve her health, but nothing worked as well as she had hoped. Then, after conducting a few tests with a doctor, they discovered something surprising: the real issue wasn't her diet or exercise routine; it was chronic dehydration. She began to drink more water throughout the day, and the results were remarkable. Her energy levels increased, her workouts became more effective, and overall, she felt healthier and more vibrant. This simple tweak was the change she needed.

This story is a great example of finding the right leverage point. What is the leverage point? In a complex system, a leverage point is a critical element or aspect where a small change can produce significant, and often disproportionate, impacts on the entire system.

For example, in a car, spark plugs are key for running the engine. If they're not working well, the car might have problems like misfiring or poor fuel efficiency. Just replacing or fixing these small parts can make the car run much better. Similarly, in a factory, the speed controller for the conveyor belt is vital. If it's not set right, it can slow down production or damage products. Fixing this can greatly improve the whole production line. These examples show how minor changes can significantly affect larger systems.

This idea applies to our careers too. It's all about pinpointing the area where a change, big or small, will have the most impact. That's what I mean by right-sized changes.

Look at Lisa, Amir, and Feng. Each of them found different leverage points for their careers. Feng's leverage point was to complete his tenure at the merged company and then go in search of new ideas and like-minded people. Amir's leverage point was to enact his missing identity and to unleash his inner artist. Lisa's leverage point was transitioning to a green marketing niche.

In my own career, at my 'what's next?' moments, the changes sometimes involved big leaps, like shifting from a corporation to becoming an independent professional. But other times, the crisis was big, and the solution was surprisingly small, yet it changed everything.

For example, a few years ago, I got burned out due to an unproductive schedule without holidays and even proper weekends. I lost my inspiration. Just thinking about work made me feel sick. My first instinct was to change everything because 'this work doesn't work for me'—sadly, that was the work I had created for myself. Eventually I realized that the problem wasn't the work, but how I was doing it—I was going non-stop, never taking breaks to recharge, and hardly ever taking a day off. Changing my grueling schedule brought my energy back. I shudder to imagine what would have happened if I had decided to give up everything then.

The 'I need to change everything' approach is risky because it may overlook simpler, less disruptive solutions that could effectively address the problem.

To figure out our right-sized change, we need to understand how our fulfillment and engagement really work. Let's break it down and take a closer look.

Key Points

- 'What's next?" moments and career turning points are golden opportunities for transformation, allowing us to catalyze positive changes.
- Make the most of your 'what's next?' moments when they occur, and even schedule them proactively.
- Identifying the right-sized change you need—a leverage point—is super important for moving up in your career.
- Watch out for the 'all or nothing' bias; it is risky because it may overlook simpler, less disruptive solutions that could effectively address the problem.

Chapter 7. When Work Isn't Working: A Case Study

In this final chapter, we are going to examine a case study of a successful yet unhappy professional, Emma. By delving into one day of her life, part by part, we'll explore the factors that drive or diminish sense of fulfillment and engagement at work.

Our case is fictional, yet it's crafted from numerous real-life scenarios. Although we'll place our character in the corporate world, you'll find that these insights are equally relevant to self-employed professionals and entrepreneurs.

Meet Emma. She is a financial manager working for a multinational company. Having devoted a great deal of time and effort to her career, she transitioned to a new company last year, ascending to a more senior leadership role. By any conventional measure, she is successful, but she doesn't feel happy at work.

Every morning, Emma drags herself out of bed, and one day she tells a trusted friend that her career isn't fulfilling anymore and she wants to change it. In response to her friend's question about what's wrong, Emma replies bitterly, 'Maybe finance was a mistake from the start. I think I need to figure out what I actually love doing..."

Have you spotted the two things here?

First, there's a big dissonance between internal feelings and external success. At some point, Emma's career stopped being fulfilling, which means that while she remains a top performer, she's become increasingly unhappy. She's on the brink of becoming a 'quiet quitter'. Quiet quitting occurs when someone psychologically disengages from their work. They might be physically present or logged into their computer, but mentally, they've checked out.

Second, from Emma's perspective, the apparent solution is a career change. This isn't surprising, as switching careers is a commonly advocated narrative. It's often the first idea that comes to mind when our passion fades and we start feeling unhappy at work.

But what if the picture is more complex, and there are far more factors at play than it seems at first glance?

Let's dive into Emma's typical working day to get the whole picture.

1. **Boss Ripple Effect**

Emma comes in early that morning, the office quiet and still, a rare moment of solitude in her bustling work environment. She settled into the meeting room and opened her laptop. She was there to put the finishing touches on a project she and her team will present today to a stakeholder. She was barely noticing the noise of a filling office as she meticulously reviewed each part of the project, ensuring every detail was just right.

However, the serenity of the morning was short-lived. The door opened and someone peered into the room. Giving a quick nod, her line manager said, "Emma, why did you ignore this morning's email from me? I expect my team to be in touch, am I asking too much?" The door closed. She felt a familiar pang of frustration.

Reflecting on a team meeting from the previous week, Emma recalled her line manager repeatedly interrupted her, questioning her methods and decisions. Her colleagues watched, their faces a mix of sympathy and discomfort. Emma's expertise, usually her stronghold, felt undermined.

These moments played back in Emma's mind as she sat at her desk, her hands hovering in pause on the keyboard. With the morning light now fully streaming in, Emma felt that the mood of the day had already changed.

Here we see the first element of Emma's work that affects how she feels—her relationship with her line manager. Needless to say, it's not a great relationship in this case.

Studies indicate that managers play a crucial role in their employees' workplace happiness.[1] People leave managers, not companies—well-known business wisdom. But there is more. A poor manager can influence not only your loyalty for a company or your role; it can also diminish your motivation, self-esteem, and overall enthusiasm for your field of work.[2] I've witnessed this countless times: a bad boss can completely reshape how you see your entire career. Their influence is powerful, often making you question everything about your professional path.

Emma thinks "maybe finance doesn't work for me, so I want to change careers", but her unhappiness and disengagement might have nothing to do with finance industry at all.

When we drag ourselves out of bed in the morning, we don't dissect that feeling into parts; we simply feel unhappy. Translating it into a systems perspective, workplace relationships, particularly with a manager, are elements that can change the entire work system. I remember a case with Serge, a project manager who loved his job but got a new manager. The job itself didn't change, but six months later, he was actively looking for new positions. When I asked what was wrong, he said work had become unbearable. "It feels like I've lost all my skills; I'm constantly criticized and micromanaged," he explained.

The relationship with a manager is a crucial element that, if it doesn't work (or if it does), can be a game changer. But this is not the only part that matter. So, let's look further.

2. **Running on Fumes**

As the late morning hours approached, Emma's energy seemed to ebb, leaving her languid. Seeking a much-needed caffeine boost, she headed to the break room. There, she became uncharacteristically short-tempered when a colleague accidentally spilled a bit of water near her. Emma immediately apologized, her frustration quickly replaced by a flush of embarrassment. "I'm sorry," she said. "It's just been hard to get any rest lately. I moved to this new place, and it's like trying to sleep in the middle of a concert of car alarms and shouting every night." Her colleague, usually accustomed to her calm demeanour, nodded understandingly.

Returning to her desk with her coffee in hand, Emma settled into her chair with a quiet sigh. "Damn, I feel like a deflated balloon," she thought, stirring her coffee listlessly. "Tired, drained... and this coffee doesn't seem to help much anymore." She took a small, unenthusiastic sip before turning her attention to the files laid out in front of her. Opening the folder for the upcoming team meeting, she tried to focus her thoughts on the agenda, pushing aside the weariness that clung to her like a stubborn shadow.

What we see here is another element, that could profoundly change the game—our physical and mental state.

Action-oriented and purpose-driven people often overlook their health as they relentlessly push forward. They live by the mantra, "I have to perform no matter what." They rarely see the connection between their physical state and their work performance. Like many, Emma was raised to ignore her own resources—her health, body, and energy levels weren't considered part of the success equation. But they absolutely are.

I once decided to run an experiment. I asked my clients to observe themselves and describe two states: when their 'battery' is fully charged and when it's running low. They were to focus on three things: how they see the world, their dreams and ambitions, and themselves. Then, I asked them to name these two modes.

Check out their answers:

Person 1: *"For me, my two modes are 'The Amoeba' and 'The Locomotive.'*

When I'm in 'Amoeba mode,' I see the world as this really bleak place. It's like, 'Ambition? Huh?' I just want to hide and not talk to anyone. I feel like I'm the one who missed all the chances, like a total loser with no way out.

But when I'm like the 'Locomotive,' everything's bright and exciting. My ambitions are huge, and I feel this pull towards other people. My head's just buzzing with dreams and ideas."

Person 2: *"I'd describe my modes as 'The Squash' and 'The Bullet.'*

In my 'Squash state,' I'm just lying there, waiting for something to happen. Mostly, I'm dreaming about not being so lazy anymore.

But in 'Bullet mode,' I'm all 'Eyes on the prize, no stopping me.' I'm super energised, motivated, and ready for some bold moves."

Person 3: *"I like to think of my modes as 'The Tortoise' and 'The Jet.'*

As the 'Tortoise,' I want to hide away in my shell, not move, not do anything. The world seems full of risks and strangers, and my dreams just feel impossible. I think of myself as having wasted my life.

Now, when I'm the 'Jet,' it's a whole different ball game. I'm up for flying into new adventures and chances. I feel like I'm in sync with the people around me, confident about what I can do. Challenges? They don't bother me; they're just puzzles to solve. And, man, my mind's overflowing with new ideas."

Have you noticed that respondents seem like two completely different individuals when they're at low versus high energy levels? They see the world differently and even view themselves in a different light.

I think of this as the 'biology of workplace happiness,' similar to Robert Sapolsky's idea of the 'biology of good and evil.'[3] He believed that our actions are heavily influenced by biological factors, such as brain chemistry, hormone levels, and neural circuitry. And there's a wealth of research out there showing how our physical and mental state can dramatically shape our emotions and overall performance.[4]

Fatigue and exhaustion really change how we perceive our work – nothing feels energizing, colleagues fail to inspire, and even our self-image seems to lose its shine. Take chronic sleep deprivation as an example – I've had clients whose passion for their work reignited once they tackled their sleep issues, and they hadn't drawn that connection before.

All of this doesn't fit into the linear cause-and-effect model of 'I'm in the wrong career, therefore I'm unhappy.' Your unhappiness might have nothing to do with your career—it could be coming from within.

In this part, we dove into another crucial element of your work ecosystem: your physical and mental state. By shifting focus from external relationships to the relationship you have with yourself, we uncovered how vital self-care is for your career satisfaction. Let's get back to Emma's story and explore another important factor from this angle.

3. In the Shadow of the Ideal Self

Emma's team gathered around the whiteboard after the meeting with key stakeholders. The atmosphere was light, filled with a collective sense of relief and a modest celebration of their project's first phase. However, Emma felt neither content nor satisfied. She wanted the results to be more impressive, as it was her first major project in this role, and she criticized herself for not achieving more.

'Here I am, with results that are merely good, not extraordinary,' she thought bitterly. 'A truly competent leader in my position would have done so much more. They would have introduced ideas that not only met the brief but redefined it, offering insights that no one else could have thought of. Their strategies would be not just effective, but visionary, setting new standards in the industry. Every decision they make would be pioneering, leaving colleagues

in awe and competitors playing catch-up. Why can't I be that leader who revolutionises our approach, who always has that game-changing idea up their sleeve?

Look at what's happening here. Like many achievers, Emma's standards are extremely high. She always carries the image of an ideal professional self in her mind and always falls short in that comparison. This constant feeling of not being good enough runs deep.

And she's not alone in this—many professionals, whether employed, self-employed, or entrepreneurs, harbor this image of their ideal self in their roles. Often, we don't even realize that we're living like undercover spies, shadowed by our ideal selves, constantly fearing exposure. We also tend to compare ourselves with the successes of others, which drains us of a tremendous amount of energy!

Perfectionists (or, in scientific terms, self-oriented perfectionists) are rarely happy at work, living in a perpetual state of 'not good enoughness.' Importantly, this feeling might not be related to the profession itself – perfectionism can make any job experience joyless. For them, the cycle of "putting effort—getting satisfaction" never closes because a person cannot derive satisfaction from his work for months or even years.

The link between perfectionism and work is a hot topic in psychology and organizational behavior studies.[5] While certain aspects of perfectionism might be beneficial in the workplace (perfectionists are more motivated on the job, work longer hours, and can be more engaged at work), perfectionistic tendencies can also clearly impair employees and entrepreneurs.[6]

Constantly chasing after perfection and the perfect performance can wear you down mentally and emotionally. Ironically, the pursuit of perfection can sometimes lead to decreased performance. That's because the stress and anxiety associated with perfectionism can impair cognitive functions like decision-making and problem-solving, which are crucial in many work environments.

In this section, we've uncovered another critical element of the work system, a less obvious factor that greatly influences our engagement and fulfillment – self-oriented perfectionism. It's amazing how much this can impact our daily work lives. Now, let's continue with Emma's story.

4. **Profession ≠ Job**

Emma's phone pinged with a message from a friend: "Here's the career advisor I mentioned. Good luck! Don't delay!"

Settling down to write her request, Emma started with a sense of firm determination: 'Finance doesn't work for me anymore. I'm ready for a major change,' she wrote. 'I'm seeking a career that brings not only success but also happiness and fulfillment.' After sending off the letter, Emma placed a sticky note on her computer. In her neat handwriting, it read, 'Follow Your Passion and You Will Never Work a Day in Your Life.' She'll find something else. Something that would ignite her excitement. Something that would make her feel like she was exactly where she wanted to be.

Let's start with a key insight about professions. Here's the thing: any profession itself (finance, design, teaching, writing, etc.) is just an abstract concept. In every career, a profession exists in a specific configuration – a unique combination of the tasks we perform, the role we hold, the company we work for, the clients we interact with and so on.

Imagine gathering ten finance managers from various companies and industries and asking them to define their job descriptions. You'd likely end up with ten distinct configurations of the finance job.

This 'specific configuration' will be our fourth element in understanding work as a system, and it plays a crucial role. Our perception of a profession is often shaped by our direct experiences with it. "Direct experience" is your firsthand, hands-on interactions with a particular job or profession. If we're not excited by those experiences, we may conclude that the profession isn't right for us.

Many people who once said 'I don't like marketing' are now happily working in marketing for different companies or with different products. That's because marketing in Company X can create a completely different experience from marketing in Company Y.

That's not the end of it, though. I've come across something pretty interesting in my practical experience. It turns out that the same task can either give us a boost of energy or totally zap our motivation, depending on how it's done. We tend to believe that if we love doing something, we'll always enjoy it under any circumstances. However, this is very contextual. The same things done two ways is not the same thing at all.

To help people understand this concept, I like to challenge them with an exercise. I ask them to take something they genuinely love doing and rearrange it in a way that makes it unenjoyable, even boring and draining. For example, take your favorite hobby and think about where, how, in what mood, and under what circumstances you would do it to strip away all the fun. One participant shared this: "I love drawing. To make it joyless, I would have to do it early in the morning while worrying about the day's to-do list. I'd constantly compare myself to those who are better than me, force myself to draw as much as possible today, and feel guilty for not being with my children. The pleasure would completely disappear if I were in a room without fresh air and stayed in one position the whole time."

What a ground for uncovering insights!

Usually, we don't realize that what makes work interesting isn't just what we do, but how we do it. I like to ask people to think about their main job tasks and tell me what is the best way to do it for them personally and what is the worst way. We're talking about things like running meetings, doing presentations, or dealing with clients—you name it. It's eye-opening because suddenly, they see that they've been tackling their work in a way that's not really working for them, and that's probably why they haven't been feeling all that motivated.

Until I realized how to reconfigure my writing process to make it work for me, I wasn't sure if writing was my thing. And the same goes for to public speaking, teaching, and conducting sessions too. I recrafted almost every important aspect of my work to make it click for me.

Have you heard about Job crafting? It's about shaping our work experience to better match our personal strengths and traits. It is like taking the reins in designing our work experience. It's not like the old-school way where your job roles and tasks are set in stone, and you just go along with the script. In the job crafting mindset, every role and task is viewed as just a draft.

That traditional way of doing things is deeply ingrained in our minds. Even when we have full control over our work, like when we're independent professionals or entrepreneurs, we might still feel like we don't truly own it. Why? Well, we were brought up thinking that there's a right way to do stuff, and it applies to everyone. We were taught about best practices, and they were supposed to be one-size-fits-all. Nobody ever really taught us to rethink how we do our work based on our unique qualities. But it's never too late to learn how to take control of your work process.

Let's go back to Emma's case. Suppose her job in its current form isn't working for her. Does this mean her whole profession is a bad fit? Absolutely not. And does it mean quitting is her only option? Definitely not. In any situation, there are always more possibilities than just sticking it out or walking away.

5. **Meaning**

As the evening shadows lengthened, Emma found herself trudging back to her apartment, the weight of the day's events heavy on her shoulders. In an attempt to unwind, she aimlessly scrolled through YouTube, her mind still entangled in the day's frustrations. It was then that she stumbled upon the CNN Hero of the Year award ceremony. The winner, a veterinarian running a nonprofit that provides medical care to the pets of homeless people, captivated her. She watched, mesmerized, as he spoke passionately about his work and the difference it made.

A profound realization dawned on Emma as she listened. Here was someone whose job was not just a job, but a calling, a source of deep and meaningful impact. A stark contrast to the emptiness she felt in her own career. The veterinarian's dedication and the evident fulfillment he derived from his work stirred something in Emma. It was as if a veil had lifted, revealing a hunger for meaning she hadn't admitted to herself before.

WHAT'S NEXT?

Emma opened her laptop and typed into the search query line 'meaningful professions'. On the second tab she began to search for jobs in the charity or animal help sector. With each click, her conviction grew stronger that her current career path and profession had been a mistake, a concession to societal expectations rather than a pursuit of her true passion.

Here, we come across another aspect of our career journey—finding meaning in our work. Emma isn't the only one; a lot of us crave that sense of meaning in what we do. In fact, research on employees has shown that when people find their work meaningful, it has a positive impact. Their performance gets a boost, they become more dedicated to their organization, and they're less likely to consider leaving.[7]

But note that Emma's line of thinking, and often what many of us first consider, is to switch to roles in charity, environmental protection, or nonprofits when searching for meaning in work. However, meaningful jobs aren't limited to just those sectors. Impactful and purpose-driven companies can be found in various fields. Contrary to what we might think, professions are rarely inherently meaningful or meaningless. It's all about context.

You might be surprised how often I hear about feelings of meaninglessness from people whose work seems absolutely meaningful – like teachers, doctors, coaches, charity workers and so on. But it does happen. We might try to use our career for good, but struggle to see the impact we hoped to make.

Take, for example, a nutritionist whose clients persistently indulge in junk food, a charity worker feeling overwhelmed by the constraints of their aid, a doctor coming to terms with the fact that not every patient can be cured, a teacher witnessing students lacking motivation, or a documentary filmmaker realizing that their film may not spark any change in the world.

I see three key factors from which people's feelings of meaning at work stem.

The first one is doing something good, purposeful, and worthwhile—everyone has their own definition of that. Second—a sense of achievement, which comes with the results you see.

Third—acknowledgment and recognition. This serves as a validation that the work has value to others.

In paradoxical examples where meaningful work feels meaningless, the first factor was present, but the absence of the second and third factors leads to a sense of futility.

As you can see, the element of meaning is complex in its nature, like a system within a system, and might have a massive influence on our sense of fulfillment.

I believe that almost any profession can be transformed into either a meaningful or meaningless experience. Emma's financial job could be just as meaningful or meaningless as any other job out there. There's no need to underestimate it just because it might not currently feel optimized for meaning. Look at Lisa's story. She was searching for a more impactful career, and her existing expertise opened doors to exciting new opportunities. It's a reminder that sometimes, the path to a meaningful career is closer than you think, and your current skills can lead you to a fulfilling future.

Summary. Seeing Work as a System

I hope Emma's story has given you a clear glimpse into why it's crucial to see the entire picture before jumping to conclusions or making any decisions. Just like in science, where every variable matters, in our careers, every element is interconnected. By understanding the full scope, we can make smarter, more informed choices that truly align with our goals and values.

From a systems thinking perspective, the notion 'Not happy? Change careers' is a classic example of linear reasoning, where one cause leads to one effect. However, linear thinking doesn't work well for complex systems like work and career.

Career is a system. It is made up of a lot of interconnected elements and every element might play its own role and shape our experience at work. Using Emma's situation as an example, we learn more about these elements and uncover how they impact our feelings at work.

In this case, we discussed several entities of work as a system:
- Relationships

- Vitality
- Perfectionism
- Work configuration
- Meaning

We left some elements out of our scope – the broader organizational and personal contexts, as well as the global context, including politics and economic situations. Each of these factors influences us in unique ways.

You can now see that linear thinking can be a slippery slope when it comes to making 'what's next?' decisions. If our primary mindset is simply 'unhappy-switch,' we risk getting caught in a cycle of endless changes rather than forging a path forward.

I also hope we've debunked the myth that simply choosing the right profession will make everything else fall into place. Our experience in any profession is defined by many contextual elements.

I aimed to highlight the strong connection between external factors and internal dynamics. Without self-awareness, we might fail to recognize how aspects like our perfectionism or health are interconnected with job satisfaction.

As we search for the right leverage point, or the right-sized change, it becomes clear that we can't define it without seeing the whole picture and understanding things as they truly are. When we know better, we do better. This leads to more informed choices.

A Message for Leaders and Companies

I've had the privilege of working with many ambitious and responsible performers, meeting them when they start pondering what's next for them. It's always a joy to witness their journey as they navigate the complexities of their careers and consider their next steps. And quite often, they find themselves weighing the decision whether to stay or leave their current employer.

I want to share what I've observed from my perspective, why your star players are packing their bag, and I hope my insights will be valuable to you.

So, why do your best people leave?

1. *They leave because of quality of relationships with their line managers.*

The role of a manager in the workplace experience is crucial. Employees who stay often do so because of the great support and good relationships they have with their line manager. Conversely, those who quit often leave because they don't feel appreciated and can't see any prospects for further development within the company.

As one of my client put it, "I joined this company full of enthusiasm, ready to contribute and grow. But it feels like I hit a wall. My boss barely acknowledges my ideas, let alone my presence. It's disheartening."

Leaders, did you know that your faith in people makes them better? When managers believe in the capabilities and potential of their employees, those employees are more likely to excel.

Numerous studies[1] show that people will rise, or fall, to the level where their superiors believe them capable. This concept is based on the psychological principle that one's positive expectations can influence another person's behavior positively, known as the Pygmalion effect. What I often see is the anti-Pygmalion effect.

People talk about feeling unsupported, misunderstood, and not trusted enough. This isn't the kind of environment where people can reach their potential and do their best work.

Your company may invest in costly strategies to retain top talent, but whether they choose to stay or leave often hinges on their relationship with one person who significantly impacts their experience at work.

2. They leave because they can't be open (and vulnerable).

"When I realized I was burned out, I tried to hold on until the last moment. Finally, I shared it with my boss," said a senior manager who experienced severe burnout after five years of delivering great results. What he heard in return was, 'So maybe you're not cut out for this role?' Later, he left the company. Of course, not because of those words alone, but I believe they played a significant role.

Here we are discussing psychological safety. Psychological safety at work means that employees feel safe to express themselves without worrying about getting in trouble. They can share their ideas, ask questions, or admit mistakes without fear of punishment. It's a concept popularized by Amy Edmondson, an

American scholar of leadership, who defines it as a climate in which individuals are comfortable being themselves and taking interpersonal risks[2].

Psychological safety is crucial for your employees' growth and loyalty to the company. Simply put, when your people feel safe, they're more willing to take risks and try new things, even if there's a chance they might mess up. Without that feeling of safety, employees might stick to what they know, never expanding their skills or trying anything new because they're afraid of failure. It's about fostering a culture where everyone is okay with being a work in progress, which is where true learning and development happen.

3. *They leave because they can't work the way they want to.*

Achievers often tell me they're missing the autonomy they crave and are dealing with micromanagement.

Letting your people craft their own work means letting them choose how to do their tasks in a way that matches their strengths and interests. It's like saying, "I believe in you to find the best way," and then giving them space to do their thing. This isn't just about making them happier (though it does that); it's also about getting better results.

Research[3] indicates that individual job redesign has a positive impact on work engagement, task performance, and career satisfaction. Job crafting strategies enable employees to shape their work environment in a way that suits them best.

I've seen lots of cases where people found greater happiness by 'reinventing' their roles. For instance, there was a sales executive who felt that her role lacked creativity and didn't fully utilize her strengths in building relationships with clients. In many cases, her only option was to change the role or the company, but with the support of her manager, she implemented a more personalized approach to client interactions. It worked out well - she felt more satisfied with her work, and her clients were happier too.

Then there's the software engineer who was on the verge of updating his CV but decided to take the initiative at his current company. He proposed a new system for project management that emphasized cross-functional teamwork and regular feedback sessions. By taking the lead and working more closely with others, he felt better about his job, and his projects went more smoothly.

Additionally, I recall the story of a marketing manager who was passionate about environmental sustainability but felt that her current role didn't allow her to make a meaningful impact in this area. Her first instinct was to change industries, but fortunately, she approached her stakeholders with a proposal to integrate sustainability initiatives into the company's marketing campaigns and products. They liked the idea, and she incorporated her passion for sustainability into her role.

When individuals craft their job, they get the opportunity to explore their full potential and experiment with new roles.

A quick word on having more control over work schedules. Many top performers are juggling their careers with family life, especially when it comes to parenting. Ambitious women on maternity leave crave flexibility. Without it, they end up leaving good jobs and later return to the workforce in less skilled, lower-paying roles just to balance work and parenting. They lose their career momentum, and you lose their potential.

I want to wrap up with a message of support for leaders. You might also deal with burnout, balance work and family, and feel the pressure of your role. Taking care of your team starts with taking care of yourself. When leaders are burnt out, it's hard to create a supportive environment. It's tough to nurture psychological safety and encourage openness. This, in turn, affects your ability to give employees the freedom to shape their roles for better fulfillment and results.

Conclusion

Lisa walked into the conference room with her laptop and notepad. She greeted the team of environmental scientists, ready to discuss the a new home battery storage systems. One of the scientists started talking and Lisa leaned in, her mind racing with ideas on how to promote these advancements to the public. This was her first campaign after a year at the new company, and she felt a familiar rush of achiever's excitement.

They brainstormed together, with Lisa sketching out concepts and strategies. She proposed teaming up with eco-friendly influencers and launching an interactive social media series to reach more people. The room buzzed as they discussed their ideas. As Lisa left the conference room, she felt a deep sense of satisfaction. She had found something that truly resonated with her.

Meanwhile, across the globe, Amir sat on the floor of his studio, trying to make sense of a branding for a startup he was trying to create. His room was cluttered with sketches, color swatches, and mood boards. The task was challenging, and at times he reached an impasse in his creative process, but Amir nevertheless felt a thrill. This project allowed for creative freedom, something he had yearned for.

He rested his chin on his hands, staring at the sketches pinned on the wall, trying to figure out how to pull everything together into a solid brand identity. By the end of the day, he hadn't cracked it yet, but that was part of the game. Despite the complexity of the task, Amir felt a deep sense of fulfillment. This was the challenge of an artist and creator—solving problems, experimenting with new ideas, and crafting something original—and he was doing exactly what he wanted to do.

That same day, Feng, along with his new partners Mike and Gigi, was interviewing a candidate for a key R&D role at their startup focused on cybersecurity. Mike, with his sharp analytical skills, asked probing questions, while Gigi's infectious enthusiasm highlighted their project's potential impact.

Reconnecting with Mike and Gigi had been a serendipitous twist. Despite months of traveling and meeting brilliant people around the globe, Feng's new partners turned out to be his old college friends. They had reconnected at a course meetup and were now ready to tackle the world together. Feng felt a familiar rush from the scale and innovation of their project, along with the associated risks and uncertainties. This was the essence of his passion—creating groundbreaking solutions with like-minded visionaries.

Lisa, Amir, and Feng made 'what's next' decisions that worked for them, but these aren't their last turning points. The same goes for you and me. We'll always be evolving, and at some point, we might find ourselves ready for the next step in our careers or facing new crossroads. Life's continual changes often bring the same big questions back into focus.

I had two goals in writing this book. First, to help you figure yourself out and decide what's next right now. Second, to equip you with the skills to navigate career turning points effectively, so that you can turn these moments into real catalysts for your future success.

Let me highlight the most important takeaways:

Principles to Remember When You're at a 'What's Next?' Point

1. **Look for the Right-Sized Change**: You're not just searching for any change but the one that fits you perfectly. This change could be a major shift, like switching industries, or a small tweak in the right area. The key is that it aligns with who you are now and enhances your career satisfaction.

2. **Always Try to See the Whole Picture**: Avoid linear thinking when tackling such a complex topic as job satisfaction job satisfaction. Consider all the interconnected elements of your situation, even those that aren't immediately obvious. These factors can have a huge impact on how you feel at work.

3. **Align with Your Vision of Success and Sense of Self**: Your career should reflect your personal vision of success and self. There's no longer a one-size-fits-all path. Craft your

career around what resonates with your own goals and identity.

4. **Learn to Sit with the Discomfort of Uncertainty:** You don't need all the answers to make a good decision. Absolute certainty is an illusion, and detailed long-term plans often crumble in a changing world. Learn to be comfortable with the discomfort of not knowing everything, embrace uncertainty.

5. **Changing the Setup May be a Game-Changer:** Any job is just an abstract idea. What really matters is the context: the tasks you do, the role you have, the company you work for, and the people you interact with. Don't give up on your profession just because your current setup isn't working, don't make this mistake.

6. **To Find the Joy of Work, Find Your Way of Work:** What makes us happy is not just what we do, but how we do it. There is no universal method for success. Discover how you perform at your best, understand yourself, and become an expert in your own productivity.

I genuinely hope this resonates with you as it has with many others I've worked with. The reality is, too many people are disengaged at work, with only 20-30% feeling happy. But think about it: we live in a time brimming with opportunities, with fewer information barriers and shifting social norms. I firmly believe that today, everyone has the power to take charge of their career and discover their own path to fulfillment.

WHAT'S NEXT?

Enjoy the journey!

I'm eager to hear how the ideas from this book are playing out in your world. If you've got feedback or stories to share, drop me a line at hello@elena-rezanova.com or connect on LinkedIn: https://www.linkedin.com/in/elena-rezanova-career/. Let's keep the conversation going and explore the possibilities together!

References

Strategy for effective reflection

1. Some of many scientific references:

Csikszentmihalyi, M. (2014). Creativity and Genius: A Systems Perspective. In: The Systems Model of Creativity. Springer, Dordrecht. https://doi.org/10.1007/978-94-017-9085-7_8

Kaplan, M. (2012). Why Great Ideas Come When You Aren't Trying: Allowing the Mind to Wander Aids Creativity. Nature, May 22, 2012. https://www.nature.com/articles/nature.2012.10678.pdf

Sio, U. N., & Ormerod, T. C. (2009). Does incubation enhance problem solving? A meta-analytic review. Psychological Bulletin, 135(1), 94–120. https://doi.org/10.1037/a0014212

Albulescu, P., Macsinga, I., Rusu, A., Sulea, C., Bodnaru, A., & Tulbure, B. T. (2022). "Give me a break!" A systematic review and meta-analysis on the efficacy of micro-breaks for increasing well-being and performance. PLoS ONE, 17(8), e0272460. https://doi.org/10.1371/journal.pone.0272460

Buckner, R. L., Andrews-Hanna, J. R., & Schacter, D. L. (2008). The Brain's Default Network. Annals of the New York Academy of Sciences, 1124(1), 1–38.

Kucyi, A., Hove, M. J., Esterman, M., Hutchison, R. M., & Valera, E. M. (2016). Dynamic Brain Network Correlates of Spontaneous Fluctuations in Attention. Cerebral Cortex.

Bressler, S. L., & Menon, V. (2010). Large-Scale Brain Networks in Cognition: Emerging Methods and Principles. Trends in Cognitive Sciences, 14, 277–290.

Elsbach, K. D., & Hargadon, A. B. (2006). Enhancing Creativity Through 'Mindless' Work: A Framework of Workday Design. Organization Science, 17(4), 470–483.

Oppezzo, M., & Schwartz, D. L. (2014). Give Your Ideas Some Legs: The Positive Effect of Walking on Creative Thinking. Journal of Experimental Psychology: Learning, Memory, and Cognition, 40(4), 1142.

Chapter 1

1. Oyserman, D. (2001). Self-concept and identity. In A. Tesser & N. Schwarz (Eds.), The Blackwell Handbook of Social Psychology (pp. 499-517). Malden, MA: Blackwell.
2. Gable, S. L., & Haidt, J. (2005). What (and why) is positive psychology? Review of General Psychology, 9(2), 103–110.
3. Leroy, H., Anseel, F., Dimitrova, N., & Sels, L. (2013). Mindfulness, authentic functioning, and work engagement: A growth model approach. Journal of Vocational Behavior, 3, 238-247.

4. Metin, U. B., Taris, T. W., Peeters, M. C., van Beek, I., & van den Bosch, R. (2016). Authenticity at work–a job-demands resources perspective. Journal of Managerial Psychology, 31, 483-499.
5. Thine Own Self: True Self-Concept Accessibility and Meaning in Life
6. Reis, G., Trullen, J., & Story, J. (2016). Perceived organizational culture and engagement: The mediating role of authenticity. Journal of Managerial Psychology, 31, 1091-1105.
7. Obodaru, O. (2016). Forgone, but not forgotten: Toward a theory of forgone professional identities. Academy of Management Journal, 60(2), 1-31.
8. Barley, S. R. (1989). Careers, identities, and institutions: The legacy of the Chicago School of Sociology. In M. B. Arthur, D.T. Hall, & B. S. Lawrence (Eds.), Handbook of Career Theory (pp. 41-65). New York, NY: Cambridge University Press.
9. Markus, H., & Nurius, P. (1986). Possible selves. American Psychologist, 41(9), 954–969. https://doi.org/10.1037/0003-066X.41.9.954
10. Lifton, R. J. (1993). The Protean Self: Human Resilience in an Age of Transformation. New York: Basic Books.
11. Obodaru, O. (2016). Forgone, but not forgotten: Toward a theory of forgone professional identities. Academy of Management Journal, 60(2), 1-31.

12. Obodaru, O. (2012). The self not taken: How alternative selves develop and how they influence our professional lives. Academy of Management Review, 37, 34-57.
13. Winnicott, D. W. (1960). Ego distortion in terms of true and false self. In D. W. Winnicott, The Maturational Process and the Facilitating Environment: Studies in the Theory of Emotional Development (pp. 140-157). New York: International Universities Press, Inc.
14. Kegan, R. (1982). The Evolving Self: Problem and Process in Human Development. Cambridge, MA: Harvard University Press.
15. Cable, D. (2018). Alive at Work: The Neuroscience of Helping Your People Love What They Do. Boston, MA: Harvard Business Review Press.

Chapter 2

1. Vallerand, R. J., Blanchard, C., Mageau, G. A., Koestner, R., Ratelle, C., Léonard, M., Gagné, M., & Marsolais, J. (2003). Les passions de l'âme: On obsessive and harmonious passion. Journal of Personality and Social Psychology, 85(4), 756–767. https://doi.org/10.1037/0022-3514.85.4.756
2. Pollack, J. M., Ho, V. T., O'Boyle, E. H., & Kirkman, B. L. (2020). Passion at work: A meta-analysis of individual work outcomes. Journal of Organizational Behavior, 41, 311–331. https://doi.org/10.1002/job.2434
3. Curran, T., Hill, A. P., Appleton, P. R., Vallerand, R. J., & Standage, M. (2015). The psychology of passion: A meta-

analytical review of a decade of research on intrapersonal outcomes. Motivation and Emotion, 39, 631-655.
4. Gilbert, E. (2015). Big Magic: How to Live a Creative Life, and Let Go of Your Fear. Riverhead Books.
5. Cable, D. M. (2019). Alive at Work: The Neuroscience of Helping Your People Love What They Do. Harvard Business Review Press.
6. Panksepp, J. (2005). Affective Neuroscience: The Foundations of Human and Animal Emotions. Oxford University Press.
7. O'Keefe, P. A., Dweck, C. S., & Walton, G. M. (2018). Implicit Theories of Interest: Finding Your Passion or Developing It? Psychological Science, 29(10), 1653-1664. https://doi.org/10.1177/0956797618780643
8. Gielnik, M. M., Spitzmuller, M., Schmitt, A., Klemann, D. K., & Frese, M. (in press). I put in effort, therefore I am passionate: Investigating the path from effort to passion in entrepreneurship. Academy of Management Journal.

Chapter 3

1. Hall, D. T. (2004). The Protean Career: A Quarter-Century Journey. Journal of Vocational Behavior, 65(1), 1–13.

Chapter 4

1. Cable, D. M. (2020). Exceptional. Chronicle Prism.
2. Sweller, J. (1988). Cognitive load during problem solving: Effects on learning. Cognitive Science, 12(2), 257-285.

3. Boksem, M. A., & Tops, M. (2008). Mental fatigue: Costs and benefits. Brain Research Reviews, 59(1), 125-139.
4. Dijksterhuis, A., & Nordgren, L. F. (2006). A Theory of Unconscious Thought. Perspectives on Psychological Science, 1(2), 95-109. https://doi.org/10.1111/j.1745-6916.2006.00007.x
5. Kahneman, D. (2011). Thinking, Fast and Slow. Farrar, Straus and Giroux.
6. Bargh, J. (2018). Before You Know It: The Unconscious Reasons We Do What We Do. Atria Books.

Chapter 5

1. Lerner, J. S., Li, Y., Valdesolo, P., & Kassam, K. S. (2015). Emotion and Decision Making. Annual Review of Psychology, 66, 799-823. https://doi.org/10.1146/annurev-psych-010213-115043
2. Han, Q., Quadflieg, S., & Ludwig, C. J. H. (2023). Decision avoidance and post-decision regret: A systematic review and meta-analysis. PLoS ONE, 18(10), e0292857. https://doi.org/10.1371/journal.pone.0292857
3. Samuelson, W., & Zeckhauser, R. (1988). Status quo bias in decision making. Journal of Risk and Uncertainty, 1, 7–59. https://doi.org/10.1007/BF00055564
4. Dugas, M. J., Freeston, M. H., & Ladouceur, R. (1997). Intolerance of Uncertainty and Problem Orientation in Worry. Cognitive Therapy and Research, 21, 593–606. https://doi.org/10.1023/A:1021890322153

5. Carleton, R. N., Norton, P. J., & Asmundson, G. J. G. (2007). Fearing the unknown: A short version of the Intolerance of Uncertainty Scale. Journal of Anxiety Disorders, 21(1), 105-117. https://arc.psych.wisc.edu/self-report/intolerance-of-uncertainty-scale-ius/

6. Azoulay, P., Jones, B. F., Kim, J. D., & Miranda, J. (2020). Age and High-Growth Entrepreneurship. American Economic Review: Insights, 2(1), 65-82. https://doi.org/10.1257/aeri.20180582

7. McLeod, S. (2018). Erik Erikson's Stages of Psychosocial Development. Simply Psychology. http://bit.ly/2Multx9

8. Age and Outstanding Achievement: What Do We Know After a Century of Research? (1988). Psychological Bulletin, 104(2), 251-267. https://doi.org/10.1037//0033-2909.104.2.251

9. Cattell, R. B. (1971). Abilities: Their Structure, Growth, and Action. Houghton Mifflin.

10. Pink, D. H. (2022). The Power of Regret: How Looking Backward Moves Us Forward. Riverhead Books.

11. Turner, V. (1974). Liminal to Liminoid, in Play, Flow, and Ritual: An Essay in Comparative Symbology. Rice Institute Pamphlet - Rice University Studies, 60. https://hdl.handle.net/1911/63159

12. Ibarra, H. (2005). Identity transition. https://flora.insead.edu/fichiersti_wp/inseadwp2005/2005-51.pdf

13. Storr, W. (2021). Selfie: How We Became So Self-Obsessed and What It's Doing to Us. Harry N. Abrams.

Chapter 6

1. Sinoway, E., & Meadow, M. (2012). Howard's Gift: Uncommon Wisdom to Inspire Your Life's Work. St. Martin's Press.
2. Stulberg, B. (2023). Master of Change: How to Excel When Everything Is Changing – Including You. HarperOne.
3. Grant, A. (2019). Think Again: The Power of Knowing What You Don't Know. Viking.

Chapter 7

1. De Neve, J.-E., Krekel, C., Ward, G., & Norton, M. (2018). Work and well-being: A global perspective. Global Happiness Policy Report 2018, February 10, 2018. Retrieved from https://happinesscouncil.org
2. Layard, R. (2020). Can we be happier?: Evidence and ethics. London, UK: Pelican Books.
3. McKinsey analysis. (n.d.). The boss factor: Making the world a better place through workplace relationships. Retrieved from https://www.mckinsey.com/capabilities/people-and-organizational-performance/our-insights/the-boss-factor-making-the-world-a-better-place-through-workplace-relationships
4. Sirgy, M. J., Efraty, D., Siegel, P., & Lee, D.-J. (2001). A New Measure of Quality of Work Life (QWL) Based on

Need Satisfaction and Spillover Theories. Social Indicators Research, 55, 241–302. https://doi.org/10.1023/A:1010986923468

5. Bai, Y., Lu, L., & Lin-Schilstra, L. (2022). Auxiliaries to Abusive Supervisors: The Spillover Effects of Peer Mistreatment on Employee Performance. Journal of Business Ethics, 178, 219–237. https://doi.org/10.1007/s10551-021-04768-6

6. Rastogi, A., Pati, S. P., Krishnan, T. N., & Krishnan, S. (2018). Causes, Contingencies, and Consequences of Disengagement at Work: An Integrative Literature Review. Human Resource Development Review, 17(1), 62-94. https://doi.org/10.1177/1534484317754160

7. Vogel, R. M., & Mitchell, M. S. (2017). The Motivational Effects of Diminished Self-Esteem for Employees Who Experience Abusive Supervision. Journal of Management, 43(7), 2218-2251. https://doi.org/10.1177/0149206314566462

8. Sapolsky, R. M. (2017). Behave: The bestselling exploration of why humans behave as they do. Penguin Press.

9. Lee, Y. S., Jung, W. M., Jang, H., Kim, S., Chung, S. Y., & Chae, Y. (2017). The dynamic relationship between emotional and physical states: an observational study of personal health records. Neuropsychiatric Disease and Treatment, 13, 411-419. https://doi.org/10.2147/NDT.S120995

10. Ratey, J. J., & Loehr, J. E. (2011). The positive impact of physical activity on cognition during adulthood: a review of underlying mechanisms, evidence and recommendations. Reviews in the Neurosciences, 22(2), 171-185. https://doi.org/10.1515/RNS.2011.017

11. Ratey, J. J. (2008). SPARK: The Revolutionary New Science of Exercise and the Brain. Little, Brown and Company.

12. Brower, V. (2006). Mind-body research moves towards the mainstream. EMBO Reports, 7(4), 358-361. https://doi.org/10.1038/sj.embor.7400671

13. Hill, A. P., & Curran, T. (2016). Multidimensional Perfectionism and Burnout: A Meta-Analysis. Personality and Social Psychology Review, 20(3), 269-288. https://doi.org/10.1177/1088868315596286

14. Flett, G. L., & Hewitt, P. L. (Eds.). (2002). Perfectionism: Theory, research, and treatment. American Psychological Association. https://doi.org/10.1037/10458-000

15. Greenspon, T. S. (2000). "Healthy Perfectionism" is an Oxymoron!: Reflections on the Psychology of Perfectionism and the Sociology of Science. Journal of Secondary Gifted Education, 11(4), 197-208. https://doi.org/10.4219/jsge-2000-631

16. Curran, T., & Hill, A. P. (2019). Perfectionism is increasing over time: A meta-analysis of birth cohort differences from

1989 to 2016. Psychological Bulletin, 145(4), 410-429. https://doi.org/10.1037/bul0000138

17. Swider, B., Harari, D., Breidenthal, A. P., & Steed, L. B. (2018). The Pros and Cons of Perfectionism, According to Research. Harvard Business Review, December 27, 2018. https://hbr.org/2018/12/the-pros-and-cons-of-perfectionism-according-to-research

18. McKinsey analysis. (n.d.). Making work meaningful from the C-suite to the frontline. Retrieved from https://www.mckinsey.com/capabilities/people-and-organizational-performance/our-insights/the-organization-blog/making-work-meaningful-from-the-c-suite-to-the-frontline

A word for leaders and for companies

1. Livingston, J. S. (2003). Pygmalion in Management. Harvard Business Review, 81(1), 97-106.

2. Shuck, B., & Herd, A. M. (2012). Employee engagement and leadership: Exploring the convergence of two frameworks and implications for leadership development in HRD. Human Resource Development Review, 11(2), 156-181.

3. Zhu, W., Avolio, B. J., & Walumbwa, F. O. (2009). Moderating role of follower characteristics with transformational leadership and follower work engagement. Group & Organization Management, 34(5), 590-619.

4. Edmondson, A. (2018). The Fearless Organization: Creating Psychological Safety in the Workplace for Learning, Innovation, and Growth. Wiley.
5. Bakker, A. B., Tims, M., & Derks, D. (2012). Proactive personality and job performance: The role of job crafting and work engagement. Human Relations, 65, 1359-1378.
6. Dubbelt, L., Demerouti, E., & Rispens, S. (2019). The value of job crafting for work engagement, task performance, and career satisfaction: Longitudinal and quasi-experimental evidence. European Journal of Work and Organizational Psychology, 28(3), 300-314. https://doi.org/10.1080/1359432X.2019.1576632
7. Tims, M., Bakker, A. B., & Derks, D. (2013). The impact of job crafting on job demands, job resources, and well-being. Journal of Occupational Health Psychology, 18, 230-240.
8. Gordon, H. J., Demerouti, E., Le Blanc, P. M., Bakker, A. B., Bipp, T., & Verhagen, M. A. (2018). Individual job redesign: Job crafting interventions in healthcare. Journal of Vocational Behavior, 104, 98-114.

Printed in Great Britain
by Amazon